ASTOUNDING TALES OF THE SEA

Astounding Tales
of the Sea

EDWARD ROWE SNOW

Illustrated

DODD, MEAD & COMPANY

NEW YORK

Third Printing

Copyright © 1965 by Edward Rowe Snow
All rights reserved

Library of Congress Catalog Card Number: 65-28323
Printed in the United States of America
by The Cornwall Press, Inc., Cornwall, N. Y.

To
Ann, 5; Nancy, 2; and Winthrop Edward, 2;
the grandchildren of my older brother
Winthrop James Snow, Dartmouth, 1914,
and his wife
Victoria;
who are the children of
Winthrop James Snow, Junior
and his wife
Sally

INTRODUCTION

Most of us are born with a curiosity concerning our fellow man. When we learn of an unusual story about him, especially if it is something to do with the sea, our interest increases.

This book is the result of many years of research into the background of its material. In addition to those stories which are centuries old, I have included many of relatively recent years. Chosen from locations all over the world, they are as far apart as the tale of the boys left to die on the ice far offshore from Newfoundland to the men who were rescued under a capsized dredge in Brisbane, Australia.

Incredible tales such as that of the man who was saved by an albatross are matched by accounts of the spies who landed at Hancock Point, Maine, and the life of hermit Quarll, discovered on a lonely South Sea Island.

All in all, I believe that you will find this volume at least approaching what I have attempted to make it, a collection of stories which can truly be called *Astounding Tales of the Sea.*

At this time I wish to express my thanks to those who helped me in the production of the book.

Editor John R. Herbert, of the *Patriot Ledger* in Quincy, Massachusetts, on many occasions during his travels all over the western hemisphere has come across items which he has forwarded to me and which subsequently appear in my books. This volume is no exception. He is always alert for unusual and even astounding stories, and at this time I acknowledge his help through the years.

The following people, in addition to those who ask for anonymity, aided me: Larry Colton; Arthur J. Cunningham; Irene Doucette; Robert Drew; Violet Durgin; Walter Spahr Ehrenfeld; Stanley Greenberg; Margaret Hackett; Marie Hansen; Reginald B. Hegarty; Melina Herron; Laurence P. Macdonald; William McIntire; Muriel McKenzie; William Pyne; Lawrence Rideout; Jan Richards of the *Courier-Mail,* Brisbane, Australia; Richard Rohe; Mary L. Roy; Capt. Robert B. Scott, U.S.C.G.; Dorothy Caroline Snow; Winthrop James Snow; Janet Sumner; Charles Taylor; Bror Tamm; F. Norman Webb; Ardes Wooster.

Institutions which proved of great help include the Mariners Museum at Newport News, Virginia, the New Bedford Free Public Library, the Massachusetts Archives, the Woods Hole Oceanographic Institution, the Massachusetts Marine Historical League, the Bostonian Society, the Boston Athenaeum, the Bangor *Daily News,* the Boston Public Library, the Massachusetts Historical Society, the U.S. Navy, the U.S. Coast Guard, the Lynn Public Library, the National Archives, the Harvard College Library, the Peabody Museum, the Essex Institute, and the American Antiquarian Society.

My wife, Anna-Myrle, kept doggedly at her task of reading copy and arranging the index, in spite of the many days of extremely hot weather last summer.

Edward Rowe Snow

CONTENTS

ix

ILLUSTRATIONS

ASTOUNDING TALES OF THE SEA

THE GREAT STORM

The greatest recorded storm in all British history, the only one ever to be made the subject of a Parliamentary Memorial, combined all the worst elements of a New England northeaster, an Asian typhoon, an Australian monsoon, a Texas cyclone, and a Florida hurricane. "The Storm," as it came to be called, left scars which were visible in countless English seaports, rivers, and countrysides for many generations.

It occurred in 1703 and followed a long series of moderate gales which had been blowing for two weeks along the English coast. On Thursday, November 25, there was a lull. All along the coast on that day the winds slowly subsided until conditions were so encouraging that many sea captains made plans to leave port.

The famous builder of Eddystone Light, Henry Winstanley, had been waiting for quiet seas so that he could visit the unusual lighthouse tower off Plymouth, as the light was in need of repairs. In view of the good weather that Thursday, Winstanley ordered his workmen to be ready to depart the next morning. At dawn they sailed from Plymouth's Barbican Steps, and the architect headed his sloop into Plymouth Sound, Friday, November 26.

There was still an "old sea" running as the men reached

their destination, but they landed at the lighthouse reef without incident.* That evening the powerful rays of Eddystone Light illuminated the area, and inhabitants alongshore recalled later that they had seen the full gleam of the light at least as late as midnight.

To their amazement, however, when the following dawn came and residents looked out to sea, the lighthouse had vanished completely. There was not the slightest indication that there had ever been an Eddystone Light! Later a few twisted and broken stumps † were identified on the ledge at low tide, but everyone out on the tower, including Winstanley, perished.

On many occasions when he had been challenged regarding the safety of his lighthouse, Henry Winstanley's retort had been that his only wish was that he could be beneath the roof of the edifice that he had built "in the greatest storm that ever blew under the face of heaven." ‡

Although many have ridiculed Winstanley's Eddystone Light because it collapsed into the sea, we should not forget that it took England's greatest storm to topple it.

On the day before the light met with disaster, hundreds of vessels had been in roadsteads awaiting the end of the two weeks of unusual gales. When the lull had come, shipping began to move again.

Suddenly, late that day, the storm resumed with increasing

---

* After years of planning, Winstanley had begun work at Eddystone, fourteen miles southwest of Plymouth, in the summer of 1696. On November 14, 1698, as Winstanley records, he "finished all and put up the light." The lighthouse worked well until "The Storm."

† The same tragic reminder of a lighthouse loss was seen the morning after the great Minot's Light storm of 1861. It was believed that this tower, located eighteen miles from Boston, Massachusetts, fell over into the sea about 1:00 A.M., April 17, 1851. Both keepers lost their lives.

‡ His widow applied for and received a pension of 100 pounds sterling providing she did not marry. She collected the pension until she died. But marry she did, a Frenchman named Tessier. This information, however, was not revealed until after her death.

fury. Harder and harder the gale blew, reaching its climax shortly before 1:30 A.M. and lasting in frenzied, terrifying intensity until 4:45 that morning. In this relatively brief three hour and fifteen minute period, the wind changed from southwest to west, from west to northwest, from northwest back to west.

After the storm, Daniel Defoe, later to be the author of *Robinson Crusoe,* decided to write a book about the disaster just as he had done about the London Plague of 1665 and the London Fire of 1666. To accomplish his purpose he sent out scores of questionnaires to almost every community and journal in England. The response was unbelievable, for hundreds and hundreds of people wrote to him.

Defoe then began to collate the material, but it was not long before he became overwhelmed by the volume of answers and the fullness of the replies. He realized that he could never include in his book, which he titled *The Storm,* all that was written to him by others about England's epochal 1703 gale.

"Some gentlemen," wrote Defoe later in explanation, "whose accounts are but of common and trivial damages, we hope will not take it ill from the author if they are not inserted. From hence it will follow, that those towns who only had their houses untiled, their barns and hovels levelled with the ground, and the like, will find very little notice taken of them in this account."

Defoe went on to state that he would not trouble the reader with details of trees blown down, parks ruined, walks defaced, and orchards laid flat. He did admit starting to count the number of trees blown down in Kent,* but gave up after he had gone beyond 17,000!

---

* Later he found conditions in Devonshire, Worcester, Gloucester, and Hereford, all of which had large orchards of fruit trees, in much worse condition than Kent.

London was a strange spectacle the morning after the storm. Everyone expected that there would be destruction, but the terrifying results of the gale were many times greater than had been feared. The waterfront was devastated, while away from the Thames entire streets of the great city lay covered with tiles and slates which had cascaded into the roads from the housetops. Because of the destruction, the price of tiles rose from twenty-one shillings per thousand to one hundred and twenty shillings, and bricklayers' labor leaped up to five shillings per day!

The average tall London chimneys proved woefully weak when the hurricane hit the city's high buildings. When the gale toppled them, in many cases their heavy weight caused them to crash right through to the basement, demolishing the houses floor by floor on their terrible journey downward.

The hurricane brought death and disaster close to Queen Anne and her royal family. At the height of the storm the Queen was taken far below the palace for safety and given shelter in an ancient but strong wine cellar. Near the palace of St. James one woman was killed by the fall of a chimney, while nine soldiers were hurt when the roof of the guardhouse at Whitehall was blown off.

The famous weather vane atop Whitehall also clattered down into the street at the height of the gale, along with many chimneys in the newer buildings at St. James. A distiller in Duke Street, together with his wife and maidservant, was buried in the rubbish of a stack of chimneys which came crashing through the floors, ending in the cellar. The wife was taken out alive, but terribly injured, while both her husband and the maid were killed.

On Fetter Lane a plasterer named Dyer and his wife had been asleep, but when the house began to shake violently, they awakened and arose at once. After he had lighted a match, Dyer was hit and killed by the fall of a stack of chim-

neys which also injured his wife, who, however, eventually
recovered.

The Bishop of Bath and Wells was killed when the chimney fell in his house. He was in his dressing gown when he
was found, probably having just arisen. His wife was killed in
bed.

Registrar John Hanson of Eaton, in London on business,
was sound asleep in the Bell Savage Inn of Ludgate Hill. His
room was on the first floor, and when the great chimney
crashed through from the roof, his bed, not in the path of
the stack, slid off the slanting bedroom floor into the gaping
hole, making a perfect four-point landing on top of the debris in the basement. His only injury was to his dignity.

In Threadneedle Street, Notary Simpson was fast asleep in
bed having heard nothing of the storm. When the gale became violent, his family went up and attempted to wake him,
but "he too fatally slept," and could not be aroused. A short
time later the chimneys fell and killed the sleeping man.

A carpenter at Swan Tavern in Whitecross was killed in almost the same manner, when a stack of chimneys fell into his
house. His wife had warned him against going to bed at the
time, as the storm was already shaking the building. Her
determination kept him up until two o'clock, but he then
retired. He was still asleep when the chimney fell through
his room, killing him while his wife, who was still up,
escaped.

Defoe tells us that the fall of brick walls in and about London "would make a little book of itself," for in certain areas
few walls escaped. Locations which suffered heavily included
St. James's, Greenwich Park, Battersea, Chelsea, Putney, Clap-
ham, Deptford, Hackney, Islington, and Hogsden. For the
next few days after the gale an "unusual air of horror" domi-
nated all those who had lived through the storm.

In one area near Oxford the local vicar had watched as a

tornado, with its awesome spout, came roaring across a nearby field. The vicar said that the only thing with which he could compare this sight was the trunk of an elephant, but the tornado was much larger.

Crossing the field, the funnel hit a great oak tree, simply tearing it to pieces. Ripping off the roof of a barn, the tornado proceeded to scatter it for miles around. Later it was learned that the twister had lifted a man off his feet and knocked him unconscious.

At Westminster Abbey the great wind stripped off the lead which covered the roof, rolling it like a piece of parchment and finally blowing it clear. St. Andrews, Holborn, Christ Church Hospital, and more than 100 other churches suffered similar damage, with the lead from several of the churches traveling incredible distances through the air.

Two turrets on the top of St. Mary Aldermary Church were blown off, one falling on the church roof. The pinnacles surmounting the top of St. Albans, Wood Street, were blown down. Part of a spire of St. Mary Ouerie's * blew off, and four pinnacles on the steeple of St. Michael, Crooked Lane, suffered similar destruction.

Strangely enough, the bridge over the Thames received little damage.

Defoe believed that the indraft of arches underneath the houses built on the bridge allowed the wind to roar through, consequently relieving strong pressure on the buildings. Certainly these houses erected over the arches did not suffer in comparison to others. When the wind in the storm blew from the southwest, it placed in the lee the east side slope of the roof of all buildings facing north and south. Thus they escaped the full violence of the wind and received little direct damage.

* Now Southwark Cathedral.

More than a hundred elms, planted by Cardinal Wolsey, in St. James's Park crashed to the ground, while acres of trees "three yards about" were lost in Moorsfields. At Baums, commonly called Whitmore House, there were more than two hundred trees blown down, and some of truly extraordinary size were broken off in the middle.

Even on the morning after the most intense period of the storm, the wind blew so hard that the women who usually went for milk to the cowkeepers in the villages around London were unable to carry their pails on their heads, as was their custom. One brave girl who started out was blown by the storm into a deep pond from which she managed to escape only after a desperate struggle. That evening it was still so windy that several of the milkmaids had their pails of milk blown off their heads!

As a result of the storm, many London houses were left looking like skeletons. It was a blessing that there was no rain for three weeks after the gale, for had a wet, rainy season followed, damage inside the exposed buildings would have been incalculable.

At Hull, well to the north of London, the storm was violent, but even that violence was moderate compared to the stupendous fury which battered the southern part of the nation. Many trees were blown down across roads all over England. As a result few avenues of travel were passable until woodsmen turned out in force, cut the trunks through, and removed them.

Countless stacks of corn and hay were either blown down or torn apart and heavily damaged. When the main body of a stack of hay stood safe, the top often became loosened by the wind. Then the hay flew about like feathers so widely separated that "there was no gathering it together." Barley and oats suffered in the same manner.

On one farm the wind lifted a great stack of corn off the

hovel or staddle on which it stood. Without dislocating the
sheaves, the giant stack described a parabola through the air
to land upon another hovel, from which the wind had
snatched up a second stack equally large. Still another stack
of wheat was taken up with the wind and set down right side
up sixteen rods away. Several stacks were taken clear from
the frame and set down whole.

"The stacks of corn in some counties, the west chiefly,
where the people generally lay up their corn in stacks, being
so damnifyed * as above, and the barns in all parts being universally uncovered, and a vast number of them overturned,
and blown down, the country people were under a necessity
of thrashing out their corn with all possible speed, lest if a
rain had followed, as at that time of year was not unlikely, it
might have been all spoiled."

Many large estates and countryseats were heavily damaged.
Their parks were completely dismantled, the trees before
their doors leveled, and their garden walls blown down. At
least a thousand estates in England suffered the loss of from
five to twenty chimney stacks. Hundreds of the same estates
lost more than a thousand trees. At least four hundred English windmills crashed to the earth and were shattered to
pieces. In many cases the windmill sails were blown around
so rapidly that the timbers began to smoke from friction,
finally setting the mill on fire.

Although a comparatively small number of people, 123,
were killed on land, well over 8,000 were lost at sea. In many
cases ships and crews were blown away, never to be heard
from again. At the time, it was believed the London Fire was
England's greatest calamity. Without question, the 1665 fire
of London was a terrible loss, with the damage reckoned at
four million pounds sterling. It is also true that vast quantities of goods were reduced to ashes in a relatively short time,

* In Defoe's day, damnify meant "bring to destruction."

when the fire destroyed 14,000 houses. Nevertheless, the fire loss was concentrated on the wealthiest part of England, whereas the 1703 storm damage reached from the Irish Sea to the North Sea and beyond. In summary, chronicler Defoe was explicit and decisive. Comparing the fire and the gale, he wrote that the damage done by this tempest of 1703 exceeded overwhelmingly that of the fire of London.

The harbor at Plymouth, the castle at Pendennis, the cathedral at Gloucester, the great church at Berkeley, the church at St. Stephen's at Bristol, the houses of worship at Blandford, at Bridgewater, at Cambridge, and many other churches all over England were terribly damaged.

In some parts of England the storm was accompanied by vivid lightning and flashes of fire. The noise the wind made was so unusual that many people mistook it for thunder. Others were sure that they had experienced a severe earthquake. No house was so strong that it did not move and shake when buffeted by the force of the wind, but it was impossible for many to distinguish whether the motion came from above or below. Rocking the strongest buildings, the gale in several places tolled the church bells in the steeples. The mighty blasts loosened the foundations of hundreds of houses, with edifice after edifice collapsing as a result.

At Cranbrook in Kent the water was salt for weeks as a result of the storm. At least sixteen miles from the sea to leeward, Cranbrook is more than twenty-five miles from the ocean to windward, the direction from which the storm must have brought the salt water. The grass was so salty that the cattle would not eat it for several days.

A physician decided that the salt must have been carried inland by the wind. Traveling soon after the storm to Tisehyrst, about twenty miles from the sea, the doctor plucked some leaves from the tops of hedges which seemed to have a white coating. When he chewed them he could taste the salt.

Several ladies of Lewes, hearing this, ate some grapes still on the vines, and they also experienced the "same relish." The grass on the neighboring downs was so salty that in the morning the sheep would not feed until hunger compelled them, and afterward drank water "like fishes."

A scientist, Anton van Leeuwenhoek, F. R. S., explained that "water may be so dash'd and beaten against the banks and dikes by a strong wind, and divided into such small particles, as to be carried far up into the land." He stated that the water, mingled with small parts of chalk and stone, hit against the windows so effectively, "that many of them became dark."

"The lower windows of my house, which are made of very fine glass, and always kept well scower'd, and were not open'd till 8 a-clock that morning, notwithstanding that they look to the north-east, and consequently stood from the wind, and moreover, were guarded from the rain by a kind of shelf or penthouse over them, were yet so cover'd with the particles of the water which the whirlwind cast against them, that in less than half an hour they were deprived of their transparency!

"During the said storm, and about 8 a-clock in the morning, I cast my eye upon my barometer, and observ'd, that I had never seen the quick-silver so low.

"There are some that affirm, that the scattering of this salt water by the storm will do a great deal of harm to the fruits of the earth; but for my part I am of a quite different opinion, for I believe that a little salt spread over the surface of the earth, especially if it is heavy clay ground, does render it exceedingly fruitful."

The great flats of the Goodwin Sands, which have figured so prominently in shipwreck accounts, are a dangerous line of shoals off Dover. Partly exposed at low water, the shifting sands here are frequently the scene of terrible disasters, and all attempts to erect a lighthouse at this location have failed.*

During the first day of the storm, the townspeople of Deal were blamed for showing "great barbarity" in neglecting to save the lives of many poor wretches. In full view of the inhabitants ashore, survivors had hung upon the masts and rigging of battered ships for hours. Others had floated back and forth upon the broken pieces of wrecks, finally going ashore at low tide upon the treacherous Goodwin Sands. They could not get across to the mainland because of the deep channels between the sands and the mainland beaches.

On the first day of the storm, the townspeople of Deal watched the sad spectacle offshore as the unlucky seamen walked to and fro upon the sands, making signals of distress. Telescopes were used by those on the shore, but in spite of their knowledge that the seamen could not save themselves, no organized help developed.

The poor sailors had a few hours' reprieve at low tide. Waiting for the death which would surely come with higher water, they realized that they would soon be engulfed and drowned by the roaring onslaught of breakers. Several boats came very near them, gathering salvage and booty, but the Deal mariners had no use for human life, completely ignoring the shipwrecked sailors. Carrying off what salvage they could, the boatmen made it a point to refuse to help the survivors, every one of whom drowned when the great waves of the sea rolled over them four hours later.

With the beginning of the storm's second day, Mr. Thomas Powell, a Deal slop-seller † by trade and at that time mayor

*Actually the Goodwins are the remains of an island called Lomea which belonged to Earl Godwine in the eleventh century. Afterward it was submerged. There is no way to walk ashore from the outlying areas of the Goodwin Sands.

† Slop-seller, a word which came into vogue in 1665, is a dealer in loose marine clothing, ready-made, and other furnishings supplied to seamen.

of the town, heard about the sailors who had been ignored by the wreckers. He decided to take action.

Hour after hour he watched vessel after vessel battered ashore on the vicious Goodwin Sands. Finally Mayor Powell appealed to the customs house officers for the use of their boats and sailors to rescue the shipwrecked seamen on the Sands. The officials, however, not only refused to help, but they would not lend their boats for others to use.

Calling his townsfolk around him, the discouraged mayor offered anyone who would volunteer to help him five shillings per head for every life saved. With this incentive several offered to go, if the mayor could find boats.

Mayor Powell now seized a customs house boat by force, although he knew this action might cause him trouble later. Having manned the government boat with a crew, Powell took away several other craft from the wreckers and salvagers, and a sufficient number of men for each boat soon volunteered.

In the remarkable rescue effort which followed, scores of lives were saved only "a few minutes" before the sailors would have drowned, and these men were brought ashore. The fast incoming tide, however, prevented the return of the rescue boats to the Sands, and as a result all who were still left stranded were swallowed up by the sea.

Now that they had been landed at Deal, Mayor Powell set about to help the survivors, who were starving, half-naked, and freezing. Since his efforts had saved them from watery graves, he now appealed to the local Queen's Agent for Sick and Wounded Seamen for funds. The haughty refusal completely disgusted him. At his own expense, he gave the survivors meat, drink, clothing, and lodging. Nevertheless, in spite of all he did, several sailors died the next day because of their injuries and exposure out on the Goodwin Sands. Ironically, having saved them, clothed them, and fed them, the mayor now was forced to bury them at his own expense. The Queen's agent still refused to give a single penny's help.

The next day the unfortunate survivors, feeling that Powell had done more than could be expected, appealed directly to the Queen's agent to help them reach London. The agent bluntly answered that he had no order, and without it he would disburse nothing. The mayor finally gave every sailor pocket money and coach passes to Gravesend. He never received the thanks of the government, though after a long wait he finally obtained the repayment of part of his money. With his wonderful example of lifesaving in mind, the government later took action on guarding the Goodwin Sands. By 1884 there were no less than four lightships in the area: *Goodwin, Gull Stream, East Goodwin, South Sands Head.*

After the storm, the river Thames was a strange sight. Hundreds of ships were blown away and only four remained. The surviving craft were left between the upper part of Wapping and Ratcliffe Cross. When the blow was at its height, no anchors, cables, or moorings would hold. Every chain across the river gave way.

With the southwest wind pushing them, the vessels had driven into the bight or bay which extends from Ratcliffe Cross to Limehouse Hole. The river, winding as it does to the dock at Deptford, runs almost due southwest. The force of the wind smashed the craft together in such great heaps that Daniel Defoe thought a man "may safely defy all the world to do the like."

Defoe went over to the Thames to see the gigantic piled-up mess of broken vessels. There lay, in hopeless jumbles, no less than seven hundred sailing ships! Many large craft had been battered into each other in the area betwen Shadwell and Limehouse. One vessel lay heeled off with the bow of another ship over her waist and the stem of still another upon her forecastle. The boltsprits * of some were driven up into the cabin windows of others.

Several vessels had their sterns tossed up so high that the tide flowed through their forecastles. Other vessels pressed so heavily on craft underneath them that before the upper craft could float, the lower ones sank to the bottom. The number of masts, boltsprits, and yards split and broken, the staving of heads and sterns and carved work, the tearing and destruction of rigging, and the squeezing of boats to pulp between other ships were beyond comprehension. Hardly a vessel had not suffered some type of serious damage.

Two ships that went down had a great quantity of goods on board. The *Russell* galley was lost at Limehouse, laden with bale goods for the Straits of Gibraltar, while the galley *Sarah* with goods for Leghorn went down at her anchor at Blackwall. Afterward salvaged and brought ashore, the *Sarah* never went to sea again, as her back had been broken. Scores of men were drowned in these two vessels, but an accurate count of those who lost their lives could never be made.

Near Gravesend several ships drove on shore below Tilbury Fort, among them five bound for the West Indies. The shore is oozy and soft here and the vessels, still erect, floated off in the next high tide. The damage was not as great as expected.

More than five hundred wherries † were lost, most of which were dashed to pieces. In two wherry disasters fourteen people were drowned on the way to Gravesend with five others losing their lives off Chelsea.

Three hundred additional craft were driven into every corner of the river, where they were sent to the bottom. More than sixty barges and lighters were found foul of London

---

* Called bowsprits today.
† Different from the present-day interpretation of the word, the wherry in that period was a large, barge-type boat.

Bridge, with sixty more destroyed between London Bridge and Hammersmith. Several score lighters and barges drove under the bridge, with most of them later sinking. In all, about one hundred lighters and barges were victims of the storm.

A great number of persons lost their lives in the Thames River but as "the Thames oftentimes submerges forever those it drowns," an accurate count could never be taken. Two watermen met their death attempting to save their lighter at Blackfriars, while a boat which capsized near Fulham drowned five people; twenty-two others are known to have lost their lives in the river there.

The tide did vital damage at the Thames River, which overflowed its banks and filled the cellars at Gravesend and on both sides in London. The alehouse keepers suffered substantial losses when a considerable amount of beer floated away.

More than 15,000 sheep drowned in the levels on the side of the Severn River near Bristol, where the sea walls were destroyed. For some time afterward the countryside lay under water two or three feet above the highest riverbank for twenty to thirty miles on both sides.

Many residents of the area around Bristol were caught by the flood. More than eighty people drowned in the marshes and the river, with several entire families perishing together.

At Bristol the tide filled the cellars, ruining merchandise worth over 100,000 pounds. The water spoiled 1,000 hogsheads of sugar, 1,500 hogsheads of tobacco, in addition to totally destroying smaller amounts of other supplies. In King Road, Bristol, the damage was almost beyond belief.

The great tides overflowing the banks of the Severn River caused a loss estimated at more than 200,000 pounds sterling. Multitudes of cattle on both sides of the river were drowned, and the lands were heavily impregnated with salt water.

The *Canterbury,* a ship carrying stores, drove on shore,

with twenty-five of her men drowning. Naval craft, including the *Richard and John,* the *George,* and the *Grace,* went to the bottom, all with heavy loss of life.

The man-of-war *Reserve* had come in to Yarmouth two days before, acting as convoy to a great fleet which had sailed to England from Russia. The captain, surgeon, and clerk of the *Reserve* had gone ashore at Yarmouth with the ship's two boats to refresh themselves and buy provisions. A few hours later they stood on a pier watching the vessel sink before their eyes. She went down about eleven o'clock, at which time the sea was too high for any help from shore, and not one person from the great man-of-war survived.

One Russian ship was driven from her anchors. Running afoul of a heavily laden collier, she sank at once, but several of her crew saved themselves by clambering to safety on board the other craft. Four small vessels were driven out to sea from this area, never to be heard from again.

At Grimsby almost all the vessels were blown out of the roadstead, and more than a score were lost. At Plymouth a relatively short time after the famous Eddystone Light disappeared, the *Winchelsea,* a homeward-bound Virginia sloop, split upon the rock where the lighthouse had stood. Her captain had sailed confidently in the direction where he thought he would find the gleam of the light, but he was never to see it. Only two sailors survived the shipwreck.

Three other merchant ships were cast away in Plymouth Road with heavy casualties. The man-of-war *Monk* rode it out, but cut all her masts by the board, as was done on scores of other craft all over England.

Many ships at Portsmouth were blown out to sea. Several of the vessels were never heard from again. The *Newcastle* later came ashore on the coast of Sussex, where she was lost with most of her crew. The *Resolution,* the pilot or advice boat *Eagle,* and the *Litchfield* prize also went down, but their crews were saved. A number of ships were driven out to sea from Cowes, one coming ashore in Stokes-Bay loaded with soldiers, most of whom were saved. Two merchant ships from Cowes disappeared forever.

After the storm, Portsmouth, Plymouth, Weymouth, and most of the English seaport towns looked as if they had been bombarded. Their damage was never accurately computed.

At Falmouth eleven sailing ships were stranded on the shore, but most of them got off again. In Barnstable Harbor a merchant ship outward-bound capsized. The pilot boat *Express* was shattered to pieces. Many ships from the Downs were driven over to the coast of France and Holland. Several saved themselves there, but others were lost.

In this gale there was one man, at least, who achieved his objective. Henry Winstanley, the builder of Eddystone Light, had wished to be at his masterpiece during "the greatest storm that ever blew." He was.

AN ASTOUNDING LIFE

Many stories have fascinated me in my thirty-year search for the unusual sea adventure. In countries all over the world astounding tales have caught my attention, and several of them have also taxed my credulity. I am more than anxious to believe the life history of a man named Ambrose Gwinett, whose career was put into a book by a reputable Boston printer and bookseller named James White.*

Because I still have doubts concerning parts of the tale I offer you now, I ask you to be the judge of what really occurred. Bookseller White speaks of the volume's "authenticity" but also states that Gwinett's life "is perhaps the most extraordinary that was ever found in the pages of history." Mr. White suggests that the book should be read and remembered as a lesson for "both Judges and Juries in the United States."

In a final criticism of the way the police and the authorities operated in 1809, James White said, "Condemnations upon circumstantial Evidence are injurious to Innocence, incompatible with *Justice,* and therefore ought always to be dis-

* White lived near the Charles Street Bridge in Boston, Massachusetts.

countenanced, especially in Cases of LIFE and DEATH." *
Ambrose Gwinett was born in 1709 at Canterbury, England. His father had a waterfront store and stocked mariner's clothing. In his writing Ambrose discusses his father:

⚓

He had but two children, a daughter and myself, and
having given me a good school education, at the age of sixteen he bound me apprentice to Mr. George Roberts, an
attorney in our town, with whom I staid four years to his
great content and my own satisfaction.

My sister being come to woman's estate, had now been
married a twelve month to one Sawyer, a seafaring man, who
having got considerable prizes, my father also giving him 200
pounds sterling with my sister, quitted his profession, and
set up a public house within three miles of the place of his
nativity, which was Deal, in the county of Kent.

I have had frequent invitations to pass a short time with
them; and in the autumn of the year 1709, having obtained
my master's consent for that purpose, I left the city of Canterbury on foot, on a Wednesday morning, being the 17th
day of September, but through some unavoidable delays on
the road, the evening was considerably advanced before I
reached Deal; and so tired was I, being unused to that way
of traveling, that, had my life depended upon it, I could not
have got as far as my sister's that night, she living, as I have
already said, three miles beyond the place.

* This argument was used in 1806, when two Irishmen were accused of
murder in Massachusetts. They were Dominic Daley and James Halligan.
Both were hanged.

With ships filling Deal Harbor and the annual fair in progress, Gwinett could not get a single room for himself at the boardinghouse, but had hopes of sharing one. The landlady approached a Mr. Richard Collins, who, dressed in a nightgown and cap, was counting money by the fire when Gwinett arrived.

"Uncle," said the woman, "this is a brother of our friend Mrs. Sawyer; he cannot get a bed any where, and is tired after his journey; you are the only one that lies in this house alone; will you give him part of yours?"

Collins answered that he was a sick man, having been blooded * that very day, but that Gwinett was welcome. The two soon retired, but Gwinett became restless and wrote as follows:

⚓

How long I slept I cannot exactly determine, but I conjectured it was about three o'clock in the morning when I awaked with a colic, attended with the most violent grippings; I attributed this to some bacon and cabbage I had eaten that day for dinner, after which I drank a large draught of milk. I found my bedfellow awake as well as myself; he asked me what was the matter; I informed him, and at the same time begged he would direct me to the necessary. He told me when I was down stairs I must turn on my right hand, and go strait into the garden, at the end of which it was, just over the sea, "but," adds he, "you may possibly find some difficulty in opening the door, the string being broke which

* In this period the doctors "blooded" (or removed blood from) their patients for fever and many other sicknesses, often endangering the patients' lives.

pulls up the latch. I will give you a penknife, with which you may open it thro' a chink in the boards."—So saying he put his hand into his waistcoat pocket, which lay over him on the bed, and gave me a middling sized penknife.

I hurried on a few of my clothes, and went down stairs; but I must observe to you, that, unclasping the penknife, to open the door of the necessary, according to his direction, a piece of money which stuck between the blade and the groove in the handle, fell into my hand. I did not examine what it was, nor indeed could I well see, there being then but a very faint moon-light, so I put them together carelessly into my pocket.

I staid in the necessary pretty near half an hour, for I was extremely ill. . . . When I returned to the chamber I was a good deal surprised to find my bedfellow gone. I called several times, but receiving no answer went to bed and again fell asleep.

About six o'clock I arose, no body being yet up in the house. The gentleman was not yet returned to bed, or, if he was, had again left it. I drest myself with what haste I could, being impatient to see my sister; and the reckoning being paid over night, I let myself out at the street-door.

Reaching the home of Mrs. Sawyer, his sister, Ambrose ate breakfast with her and her husband. At eleven o'clock three horsemen galloped up to his sister's house, dismounted, and grabbed him.

"You are the king's prisoner," shouted one of them, and then took the trouble to explain to Mr. Sawyer that Gwinett had committed a murder and robbery. Protesting his innocence, Ambrose was carried back to Deal, with his brother-in-law and a friend accompanying the group.

Gwinett was taken at once to the house where he had slept the night before. Met at the door by a crowd of shouting people, he listened as they began chanting, "Which is he? Which is he?" He was now accosted by the wife. "Where hast thou hid his money, and what hast thou done with his body? thou shall be hang'd upon a gallows as high as the May-pole."

Gwinett was brought into a private room where he was given a sort of eighteenth-century third degree. He was asked where he had put the money and how he had disposed of the body. Gwinett shouted out in anguish, "What money, and whose body?" They then charged that he had killed the person whose bed he shared the preceding night for the sake of a large sum of money. Gwinett fell down on his knees, calling God to witness he knew nothing of the murder or robbery.

Taken upstairs, he watched as they examined the sheets, pillow, and bolster, all of which were dyed with blood. A person in the room, whom Gwinett did not know, then spoke up.

"Young man, something very odd must have past here last night; for lying in the next chamber I heard groanings, and going up and down stairs more than once or twice."

Gwinett explained that he had been ill the night before and had been up and down the stairs himself. Several men then grabbed him and emptied his pockets. With a clatter the penknife and the piece of money tumbled upon the floor.

Seeing them, the woman instantly screamed out, "O God! There is my uncle's penknife! Here is what puts the villain's guilt beyond a doubt; I can swear to this William's and Mary's guinea; my uncle has long had it by way of a pocket-piece, and engraved the first letters of his name upon it."

She then began to cry while Gwinett could do nothing but continue to call heaven to witness that he was innocent. Further bloody evidence of his alleged crime was revealed at the backhouse or necessary, which was located a few feet over the tidal water. The constable noticed blood in the necessary.

"Here," said the constable, "after having cut the throat, he has let the body down into the sea. Then it is in vain to look for the body any further, for there was a spring tide last night, which has carried it off."

Gwinett was soon brought before a Justice of Peace, after which he suffered a long imprisonment in the county town of Maidstone. For some time his family, believing him innocent, put an advertisement in the *London Gazette,* offering a reward to any person who could give tidings of Mr. Richard Collins, either alive or dead. No information, however, of any kind came to hand, and gradually even his family lost faith.

At the assizes, he was brought to trial. Because the circumstantial evidence was so strong against Gwinett, he was sentenced to die.

In the hushed courtroom the judge told the prisoner that he was to be carried in a cart to a gallows erected in the town of Deal the "Wednesday fortnight following" and there be hanged before the innkeeper's door where he had committed the murder. Then Gwinett's lifeless remains would be hung in iron and chains within a short distance of his sister's house.

On the Monday preceding the fatal day when an end was to be put to Ambrose's miseries, he was called down into the court of the prison. Hoping to receive some sort of good news, he was shocked to find a blacksmith there to take measurements for the irons * in which he was to be hung after the execution!

"A fellow prisoner appeared before me in the same woeful plight (he had robbed the mail) and the smith was measuring him when I came down; while the jailor, with as much calmness as if he had been ordering a pair of stays for his

---

* Two centuries ago, noted criminals, after death, were hung with chains and iron bands around their remains to warn others against crime.

daughter, was giving directions in what manner the irons should be made, so as to support the man, who was remarkably heavy and corpulent."

From that moment on Gwinett spent his time alone in prayer and meditation. At length Wednesday morning came. At about six o'clock he was put into the cart of death. It was a day of wind, rain, and thunder, such as the inhabitants had not seen for years. When they arrived at Deal, the storm became so violent that the sheriff and his officers could scarcely stay on their horses. Gwinett, however, by this time was "in a manner insensible" to every thing around him.

Because of the terrible storm * the sheriff told the executioner to hurry the hanging. As a result, in the pelting rain, no slipknot was tied. Long after the sheriff's officers had gone, Gwinett's brother-in-law stayed watching the hanging man as the rain poured down. He observed the executioner when he came to put the irons on his brother's body. It was found that a mistake had been made and that the irons of the other prisoner, much too large for Gwinett, had been sent instead. To make the body fit the bands, the executioner stuffed rags inside the hoops. Gwinett was then taken to a field near the Sawyer residence where he was exhibited upon a gibbet, which had already been prepared.

The cloth over his face soon blew away because of the violence of the gale. When the wind hit Gwinett's bare face, it brought him back to consciousness. Because of the faulty hanging he had not been dead at all and gradually came to his senses.

The gibbet had been placed at one corner of a small common field, where the Sawyer cows usually were pastured. About this time the lad who took care of them came to drive them home for evening milking. The creatures, which had

* Years later, at Worcester, Massachusetts, Bethsheba Spooner and her paramours were hanged in a similarly violent thunderstorm.

been feeding almost under the place where Gwinett was hanging in chains, brought the boy near the gibbet. Naturally the lad stopped to look at the spectacle and noticed that the cloth was off Gwinett's face. At the very moment when he looked up he saw Ambrose open his eyes and move his underjaw.

The poor lad, overwhelmed at the apparition of the body coming back to life, collapsed under the gibbet. He soon picked himself up and ran to the Sawyer residence where he stammered out his story. Sawyer did not believe this incredible tale at first but decided that he should investigate the unlikely story that a hanged man had come back to life. By the time he reached the field Gwinett had recovered to such an extent that his groans were audible.

It was now dusk. The first thing they ran for was a ladder, which one of Sawyer's men mounted. Putting his hand above Gwinett's stomach, he felt a strong heart beat. It was impossible, however, to detach the prisoner from the gibbet without cutting it down, which was finally accomplished. In less than half an hour, having freed him from his irons and chains, they had Gwinett "blooded" and in a warm bed in his sister's house.

Amazingly, although eight people knew that he was still alive, Gwinett remained three days in the house undetected by the authorities. No one revealed his presence.

Having been miraculously saved from the gallows, the condemned man could not stay in England for a return performance. In this dilemma, a fortunate circumstance presented itself.

Two of the chief officers of a privateer that had been preparing for a cruise and was now ready to sail were visiting Gwinett's brother-in-law. Hearing of the circumstances, the captain kindly offered to take Gwinett aboard with him, and they left within a few hours. By the time he was far at sea,

Gwinett began to recover his health, and as the weeks went by, he was soon his old self again.

The weeks became months, and half a year soon elapsed. While off Florida, then part of Spain, they unfortunately fell in with a squadron of Spanish men-of-war. After a brief encounter they had to surrender without "striking a stroke." They were all brought to Havana as prisoners. By this time Gwinett was almost weary of life and would have been very glad to have ended it in one of the loathsome dungeons for which Havana was noted. The enemy stowed him and forty others in the deepest dungeon available. After three years in close confinement they were all let out to be put on board transports for Pennsylvania and England.

This was a disagreeable sentence for Ambrose Gwinett, who took it for granted that to return home meant another trip to the gallows:

⚓

Being now therefore a tolerable master of the Spanish language, I solicited very strongly to be left behind; which favour I obtained, by means of a master of the prison, with whom during my confinement, I had contracted a sort of intimacy; and he not only took me into his house as soon as my countrymen were gone, but in a short time, procured me a salary from the governor for being his deputy.

Indeed, at this critical time, the office was by no means agreeable. The coast had been long infested with pirates, the most desperate gang of villains that can be imagined, and there was scarce a month passed, that one or other of their vessels did not fall into the governor's hands, and the crews as constantly were put under my care.

Once I very narrowly escaped, being knocked on the head by one of the ruffians, and having the keys wrested from me;

another time I was shot at. 'Tis true in both cases the persons
suffered for their attempt, and in the last I thought a little
too cruelly; for the fellow who let off the carabine,* was not
only put to the torture to confess his accomplices, but afterwards broke upon the wheel, where he was left to expire, the
most shocking spectacle I ever beheld with my eyes.

One day a ship arrived with nine prisoners from Port Royal,
another Spanish settlement on the coast. Ambrose was standing in the street as the prisoners, with a guard of soldiers,
were coming up from the port to the governor's house. Something in the face of one of the prisoners reminded him of a
man with whom he had been acquainted. An hour later they
were all brought down to the prison where Gwinett had an
opportunity of taking more notice of the man who had attracted his attention.

Finally he reached his unbelievable conclusion. This man
must be the person for whose supposed murder he had suffered so much in England; of this he was sure. The thought
was so strong in his mind that he did not sleep a wink the
whole night.

In the morning after their arrival, I told them that if
any of them had a mind to walk about the town, I would
procure them permission to go along with them. This man
said he would go, and it was what I wished.

Three other prisoners that went along with us, walked a
little in advance. I now took the opportunity, and looking in
his face, "Sir," said I, "was you ever in Deal?" I believe, that

* A carabine was a musket of the period.

at that instant, he had some recollection of me; for putting his hand upon my shoulder, tears burst into his eyes.

"Sir," says I, "if you were, and are the man I take you for, you here see before you one of the most unfortunate of human kind; is your name Collins?"

He answered it was. "Richard Collins?" said I. He replied, "Yes."—"Then," said I, "I was hanged and gibbeted upon your account in England."

After our mutual surprise was over, he made me give him a circumstantial detail of everything that had happened to me in England from the moment we parted. I never saw any man express so much concern as he did, while I was pursuing the melancholy story of my adventures; but when I came to the circumstance of my being hanged, and afterwards hung in chains, I could hardly prevail upon him to believe my relation.

When I had done, "Well," said he, "young man [for I was then but in my five and twentieth year; Mr. Collins might be about three and forty], if you have sustained misfortunes upon my account do not imagine (though I cannot lay them at your door) that I have been without my suffering. God knows my heart, I am exceedingly sorrowful for the injustice that has been done to you, but the ways of Providence are unsearchable!"

"When you left me in bed," said he, "having at first wakened with an oppression I could not account for, I found myself grow extremely sick and weak; I did not know what was the matter, when accidentally putting my hand to my left arm, in which I had been blooded the morning before, I found my shirt wet, and in short, that the bandage having slipped, the orifice was again opened, and a great flux of blood ensued. This immediately accounted for the condition I found myself in.

"I thought, however, that I would not disturb the family

which I knew had gone to bed very late. I therefore mustered all my strength, and got up with my night gown loose around me, to go to a neighboring barber, who had bled me, in order to have the blood stopped and the bandage replaced. He lived directly opposite to our house; but when I was crossing the way, a band of men, armed with cutlasses and hangers, came down the town and seizing me hurried me towards the beach.

"It was in vain that I begged and prayed to be released; they soon silenced my cries. At first I took them for a press-gang,* but afterwards found they were a gang of ruffians, belonging to a privateer, aboard of which they immediately brought me. However, before I got thither, the loss of blood occasioned me to faint away.

"The surgeon of the ship, I suppose, tied up my arm; for, when my senses returned, I found myself in a hammock with somebody feeling my pulse. The vessel was then underway. I asked where I was. They answered I was safe enough.

"I immediately called for my night gown, it was brought me; but of a considerable sum of money that was in the pocket of it, I could get no account. I complained to the captain of the violence that had been done me, and of the robbery his men had committed; but being a brutish fellow, he laughed at my grief, and told me, if I had lost anything, I should soon have prize money enough to make me ample amends.

"We were taken by the Spaniards; and by adventures parallel to your own, you now see me here, on my return to our native country, whither if you will accompany me, I shall think myself extremely happy!"

* Gangs which searched the streets looking for possible sailors for the navy.

There was now nothing to prevent Ambrose from going back to England; for the man he was supposed to have murdered had appeared. A ship was ready to sail for Europe in eight or ten days, and in it they determined to embark. After bribing the guard with a substantial payment from a fund he had saved for just such a purpose, Gwinett escaped with Collins.

The same night, November 18, 1712, eight pirates escaped from jail and stole a boat which they sailed to a cove down the coast.

Meanwhile, having made all preparations, Gwinett sent his trunk aboard the *Nostra Senora,* a merchant ship, bound for Cadiz. Her master was Michael Deronza. The vessel, which was to sail that night, lay in the road about three miles from the town. About seven o'clock in the evening, while Ambrose was getting ready to leave, a lad came up and said that the ship had been waiting half an hour for him at the port and that Mr. Collins was already on board.

Gwinett ran into the house for a small bundle and made what haste he could to the quay. Here he found that the boat had already put off, leaving word that Gwinett should overtake them at a little bay about a mile beyond the town. Running along the shore he soon sighted a boat to which he shouted as loud as he could. They put about and took him aboard. When they were fifty yards from land, he looked in vain for his friend Mr. Collins. He had made a mistake. Instead of getting on board his boat, which he now saw a considerable way ahead, Gwinett had gone aboard the boat belonging to the pirates who had escaped from prison.

He was forced to join their "brethren" or be killed, and he chose to keep alive. Soon other craft were captured, and more and more sailors joined the pirates. Gwinett remained among them almost four years, during which time there were no less than eleven killings aboard ship.

Their captain was an Irishman, Bryan Walsh, a most vicious and unprincipled villain, although in spite of this he became a very good friend to Ambrose.

In one of their cruises the pirates sighted a Jamaican ship and hoisted out their black colors. Soon they came up alongside, and in the fighting which followed one of the pirates was killed. After the resistance ended, Captain Walsh ordered the whole crew massacred because of the pirate's death, and the seven survivors were executed.

Descending into the hold, the pirates found the Jamaican craft's cargo was sugar and rum. After removing it, they returned to the pirate stronghold ashore.

The prize rum, which was of an exceptionally potent nature, was consumed by the men in such quantities that in a little more than ten days it was gone! Seven men had drunk themselves to death, including Captain Walsh.

On his deathbed, the captain called Gwinett aside and told him that he was leaving all his wealth to him. On the captain's death, Ambrose decided it was time to become an honest man, and suggested to the others that they do likewise. They agreed to the proposal with more alacrity than he thought they would. Immediately they began to put aboard from the island all the worldly wealth they had accumulated.

They weighed anchor on the third of August. For three days the weather was good, but on the fourth a storm began to threaten. The storm became a gale, and about three o'clock in the morning they were obliged to heave to under bare poles. The sea was running so exceedingly high that it was impossible to keep their lights on. In the hurricane then raging, they threw overboard first the guns and then, with understandable reluctance, the chests of treasure. In this way

Ambrose was once more reduced to his original state of relative poverty.

As daylight appeared the storm subsided. That afternoon the boatswain came up to Ambrose and said, "Damme, master Gwinett, you have brought us all into a pretty hole here; if it had not been for you, we should not have taken this trip, and lost the substance we have been working for so many years."

Then, without further ceremony, the boatswain and three others seized Gwinett by the neck and his waistband and threw him into the sea. As he came to the surface, he watched the ship sail out of sight. The storm had left the ocean littered with wreckage. Among several objects in the water he sighted a swamped boat which had evidently been washed overboard from some other craft in the storm. Swimming slowly to it, he clambered in.

When moderate weather followed the tempest, Gwinett found no trouble managing his small craft. Thirty hours later a sail appeared, a Spanish carrack bound for Port Royal, which took him aboard. Landing at Port Royal, he was seized by the authorities and put in jail. He remained in prison for two years until a summons came to bring him over to Cadiz in old Spain in order to testify at a pirate trial.

After his arrival in Spain, he was again confined for many months. The criminals were brought to trial, and Ambrose was convicted with the other pirates for his part as a member of the brethren. All were sentenced to serve in galleys for the remainder of their lives.

Ambrose worked on the galleys several years as a slave at the oars. At last his craft was ordered to sea against an Algerian rover that was pillaging the coast, but instead of sighting a single enemy ship, the galley encountered three Algerian vessels.

In the fight with the Algerian pirates, most of the galley

crew were killed and the remainder taken as prisoners. At the height of the battle, Gwinett was seriously wounded, losing one of his legs as a result of the action.

"After this I passed a long and painful slavery in Algiers till, with many other English captives, I was released by agreement between the Dey of Algiers and his Britannic Majesty's Agent."

Suffering many additional trials and tribulations, Ambrose Gwinett returned to England in the year 1730. The first thing he did was to inquire after his relations, but all those nearest to him were dead. He learned that Mr. Collins, for whose murder he had been hanged, had never reached England, probably dying at sea.

"Though not an old man, I was so enfeebled by hardships and worn out with grief and disappointment, that I was unable to work; and being without any manner of support I could think of no way of getting my living."

For a long time he swept the sidewalks between the Meuse Gate and Spring Garden, Charing Cross, receiving a pittance for this task.

In the year 1758 a budding young Irish dramatist named Isaac Bickerstaffe interviewed Ambrose Gwinett at the time the latter was suffering abject poverty in London. Bickerstaffe, who eventually died in extreme poverty on the continent, is responsible for the first draft of Gwinett's remarkable life.

We cannot state how Gwinett passed his final years, but this unusual Englishman indeed had a strange career. Hanged for a murder he did not commit, coming back to life to discover his alleged victim years later, and then turning pirate through no fault of his own—surely Gwinett deserved to pass his final days in peace and happiness. However, there is not the slightest proof that this was the case.

QUARLL THE HERMIT

In the year 1943 I was recuperating in England from my relatively brief participation in the 1942 North African Invasion as a member of the 12th Bomber Command, U.S.A.A.F. We had been landed at Bristol, England, from Mers-el-Kebir, and were put into Frenchay Hospital outside of Bristol.

One day a group of us who were showing improvement were allowed to go into Bristol for a visit. As I was anxious to purchase film for my camera, I stepped into a chemist's shop, or drugstore, where I met for the first time Mr. Fred Penfold, the proprietor, who sold me a roll of the precious film. Thus began a lasting friendship which was not terminated until his death several years ago.

During my stay at Frenchay Mr. Penfold drove me around the area as far as his petrol ration would allow. He soon discovered my interest in unusual sea stories, and he promised that there was one which would more than hold my attention. One day he took me to the public hall where records were on file concerning a Bristol merchant, Edward Dorrington, who had visited a South Pacific island more than two centuries before.

It was evident that the manuscript material originally contained more than a hundred thousand words written both by the Bristol merchant and by a Philip Quarll, the hermit of an island in the South Pacific. Because of World War II bombing by the Germans, the original manuscript had been removed to a safe location, and what I was allowed to read was an abridged account of about 58,000 words, which had been secured in a beautifully embossed leather binding.

I shall never forget Mr. Penfold's thoughtfulness in making it possible for me to read the Dorrington-Quarll manuscript. The story follows:

While sailing back to England in the year 1724, Edward Dorrington was becalmed in the South Pacific near an island whose beauty and grandeur attracted him. Apparently, the island had no easy means of access on account of the terrifying surf breaking almost continually on the rocky ledges surrounding it.

Because the weather was remarkably calm, however, Dorrington and a friend named Alvarado decided that landing at the island was a challenge and engaged an oarsman to row them in to the ledges.

The oarsman detected a cleft in the outer rocks and rowed through. Twenty minutes later all three men were ashore. With anticipation they walked inland and soon reached a delightful valley which they explored for several hours. They discovered a thatched house near a deep forest, but there was no one inside or around the residence. Dorrington and Alvarado posted their boatman in the house and began a search for the residents of the island. Later they sighted an old man with an unusual two-legged creature some distance away and walked toward them.

After a short interval they saw the man close at hand. The venerable patriarch wore a white beard which concealed his naked breast, while white hair covered his shoulders and hung down to his loins. His companion was a monkey!

Sighting the men, the patriarch dropped the hatchet and
bundle of sticks he was carrying and ran up to Mr. Dorrington.

"Dear countryman—for I heard you speak in English—by
what accident did you come here? The approach to this place
is defended by a thousand perils and dangers, and not to be
come at but by a narrow escape from death. Are you shipwrecked?"

"No, thank God," answered Dorrington. "We landed because of the extreme calmness of the sea. But, pray, how did
you get here?"

"I was shipwrecked," answered the man, whose name
turned out to be Philip Quarll, "thanks to my Maker, and
was cast away. Were I made emperor of the universe, I
would not be concerned with the world again, nor would you
require me, did you but know the happiness I enjoy out
of it."

The old man was extremely convincing in his philosophy.
He explained that he had plenty to eat and drink as well as
clothes in abundance.

"This is a second Garden of Eden; only here is no forbid-
den fruit, nor woman to tempt a man. . . . I was but eight and
twenty when I was cast away, and that is but fifty years ago.
Indeed if I lived as you do that dwell in the world, who hurry
on your days as if your end came on too slow, I might be
accounted old."

Quarll then challenged Dorrington to move a boulder
which weighed several hundred pounds. Attempting to dis-
lodge it, Dorrington barely budged the rock. The old man
went up to the stone, lifted it, and threw it several feet.

"Come," said Philip Quarll, "let us make much of that
little strength we have left. It is now past noon. Therefore
let us lose no time, but hasten home to get our dinner ready.
This island," he explained, "is inhabited with monkeys and

myself, but nobody else, thank God. Otherwise, I can tell you, I should hardly have lived so long."

Philip Quarll then explained that he had trained his monkey to do many tasks for him. Quarll told how one day he found the monkey near his residence and fed him. Since then the beast had acted like a devoted dog, but having hands, was able to learn many tasks around the house. Years before Quarll had had another, better-loved monkey.

"About eight years ago, which is the time I have had this present beast, I was walking under one of the clusters of trees where the green monkeys live, which being the largest and most shady in the island, I took the most delight therein; as I was walking, at a small distance from me this creature dropped off a tree, and lay for dead, which being of the gray kind, made me wonder less at the accident.

"I went and took him up, and accidently handling his throat, I opened his windpipe, which was almost squeezed closed by that which took him, which my sudden coming prevented from strangling quite. I was extremely well pleased at the event, by which I got what my past cares and diligence never could produce me.

"Having pretty well recovered its breath, and I seeing no visible hurt about it, I imagined that I soon might recover it quite; so hastened home with it, gave it warm milk, and laid it on my bed; so that with careful nursing I quite recovered him; and with good keeping made the rogue thrive to that degree, that he has outgrown the rest of his kind."

"No question, sir," said Dorrington, "having taken such pains with him, you love him as well as his predecessor."

"I cannot say so, neither," replied the old man, "though I love the creature; but its having the ill fortune to be of that unlucky kind which was the death of my dear Beaufidelle,* in a great measure lessens my affections. Besides, he falls so

* Beaufidelle was his best-loved monkey.

short, both of his merit and beauty, that I must give the deceased the preference; and was it not for his cunning tricks, which often divert me, I should hardly value him at all; but he is so very cunning and facetious, that he makes me love him, notwithstanding I mortally hate his kind."

Philip Quarll then laid the tablecloth which was made of part of a ship's sail, setting on it three shells, each about as large as a middle-sized plate but as beautiful as any pearl Dorrington had ever seen.

"Gentlemen, if you can eat off shells, you are welcome. I have no better plates to give you."

Dorrington and his friend expressed themselves as being delighted to enjoy their repast from the shells.

The first dish served was soup, which was partaken of by one spoon made of shell. The fragrant smell of the soup excited Dorrington's appetite. Later he said he had never eaten anything comparable to it, even at Pontac's.*

The soup was really a stew made of an animal Quarll had caught that morning and several sorts of herbs, which reminded Dorrington of artichokes, asparagus, and celery. There were also bits of roasted roots in it instead of toasted bread, making it taste like chestnuts. He also noticed green peas in the stew of an "extraordinary sweetness."

"Now these peas which have so much raised your surprise are indeed the growth of this island, though not its natural product, but the gift of Providence, and the fruits of labor and industry. I have tilled the ground; Providence procured the seed; † nature gave it growth, and time increase; with seven peas and three beans, I have, in four years' time, raised feed enough to stock a piece of ground, out of which I gather yearly a sufficient quantity for my use, besides preserving fresh seed."

---

* A famous English eating establishment of the early eighteenth century.
† Quarll had discovered the dried peas and beans in a pocket of his clothes.

The others having eaten sufficiently of the soup, Quarll fetched in boiled meat and oyster sauce, which he brought in another shell similar to that in which the soup was served, but somewhat shallower. The meat was as delicious as "house-lamb." The dinner was embellished later by roast beast, mushrooms, and pickles. Not only did the pickles exceed anything that Dorrington had ever tasted in Europe, but later in the meal an outstandingly delicious cheese was served.

Philip Quarll now asked about his native country of England which he had left fifty years before. Dorrington gave him a long history of political and economic developments there. At the end of the meal they drank good King George's health in a kind of wine made from fermented root juices. This toast was followed by another to the royal family and prosperity to the church.

Philip Quarll now decided to give his company a short lecture including ten commandments which "if rightly taken may be of use to you." He seemed especially antagonistic to women in general, as he was very emphatic on his third commandment, which was, "Waste not your substance and vigor on women, lest waste and want be your reward. Secrets are not safe in a woman's breast; it is a confinement the sex cannot bear."

Dorrington thanked him at the conclusion of the lecture and said that he would consider Quarll's ten commandments at a future date. The sun by this time was sinking in the west, and Dorrington informed the old man that he would have to leave. Indeed unhappy at the parting, Philip told them he would take them over to the pond first and then back to the house.

When they reached the edge of the pond, Dorrington was surprised at the transparency of the water. Looking down into the clear depths he saw what appeared to be large rubies, emeralds, and other colored stones. The old man now took him by the hand.

"Come," said he, "I will keep you no longer; night comes on apace, and the retreat from this island is dangerous. Therefore, I would have you improve the short remains of the day, to avoid the dangers the darkness of the night may lead you into; so let us go home, that I may give you the memorial I have promised you, and then my blessing, and hearty prayers for your safe departure, and happy arrival." So they went to his habitation where he gave Dorrington a bundle of tightly rolled parchment.

Philip Quarll now took Dorrington into his arms and embraced him with tenderness, explaining that after Dorrington went it would be "a renewing" of his past grief. Ten minutes later, Dorrington and his two companions rowed away from the island. They left just in time, fortunately, because the wind was beginning to rise and the sea starting to break against the ledges. They reached the ship, waved farewell to Quarll, and sailed away. After a rough voyage Dorrington landed at Panama on May 26, 1724. Leaving there June 5, his ship passed through a violent storm but weathered it successfully. Dorrington reached England on January 3, 1725, and began a careful study of the Quarll document.

He discovered that Quarll found almost everything necessary for human life on that small island; and he "who then thought of nothing but immediately perishing in the most miserable condition, has lived, by the help of divine Providence, in a safe and plentiful manner; and is now so inured thereunto, that he despises the popular world, and its vanities; he also considers its pompous glory to be of no more substance than a shadow; and that there is no felicity on earth, unless in solitude."

The actual manuscript of this English hermit, which was

given to Edward Dorrington on the island in the South Seas, is a long one. Therefore we are limited to emphasizing only what may appear to be the important, interesting facts of his life.

Philip Quarll, the son of Thomas Quarll, was born in 1647 in the parish of St. Giles, England. When the family became poor, a well-to-do neighbor adopted the child for her own. Unfortunately the worthy lady died suddenly, but there was enough money for young Philip to keep going for the next four years to the school in which she had started him. He made himself "a complete master of the grammar, writing, and arithmetic" and became an outstanding singer.

Later he left school. Soon after his departure he made the friendship of James Turner, a housebreaker, who led Quarll astray.

Luckily Turner was apprehended before long for a robbery he had committed some time earlier and was put in jail. Young Philip, as his companion, was imprisoned. When the judge learned that Philip had never been guilty of robbery, he was allowed to go free, while Turner was hanged. Philip's poor widowed mother learned of the incident and was grieved to find that her son had fallen on evil days.

Philip decided to go to the town of St. Catherine's, where he might be able to sign on as a cabin boy on a ship, and so he said good-bye to his mother. When he reached St. Catherine's, the captain of a vessel bound eventually for the East Indies took a particular fancy to him and asked him if he would like to go to sea. The gentle manner in which he spoke to Philip made the lad interested in going on the voyage. The captain gave him half a crown to spend with his mother when he returned to his home for a visit, and two days later he sailed away aboard the ship.

While at sea Philip made a good impression on everyone in the crew and was often with the man at the helm. He soon learned how to use the compass, and by constant application qualified himself as a real sailor. For the next few years he sailed to many ports of the world.

One day the ship was at anchor at Gravesend. A few hours before sailing on a long voyage to the Pacific the crew all went over for a final drink at the alehouse.

There they "set their brains floating in strong drink" for six hours, having "lost the rudder of their reason," and "run headlong upon those quicksands" where most of them lost all they had before they hit the dock.

Finding women companions, the other sailors left Quarll by himself. He then became interested in a young lady named Mary, who was considerably older than he. An impetuous romance developed, and after a fast conquest, she decided that they should get married. Nearby there was a chaplain from a man-of-war who married them, at "that critical minute." The ship then sailed without Philip, who now had problems ashore.

The newly married couple did not have much money, but Philip attempted to make a go of the union. After a hectic life with Quarll, however, Mary became seriously ill and died a few weeks later.

After waiting a few months, Quarll found himself fascinated with a girl named Sally. She in turn expressed herself as willing to marry Philip, and the two were joined in holy matrimony early the following year.

Eventually tiring of life ashore, Philip learned of a vessel about to sail for the South Seas. He told Sally of his plans for an ocean voyage, and she informed him that she was also interested in making the trip if it could possibly be arranged.

Since the vessel's captain had been first mate of the ship to which Quarll had formerly belonged, Philip decided to approach him. Quarll told the captain a little about his past life, including the death of his wife and his second marriage, and the captain became interested.

The captain explained that he himself had been ship-wrecked twice, once upon the coast of Guinea where he lost his ship and cargo with but five men saved. The other time he was homeward-bound from the East Indies when his craft was driven on the coast of France. He informed Quarll that if the young man had any money to invest, he could put it into woolen manufacture and cutleryware and then he could sell it at some port during the voyage. He told Quarll that Sally could come along.

Quarll then went to Sally and explained what he had been doing and where he intended to go, and Sally said, "All right, I'll come along on the ship." So Quarll bought all the goods about which the captain advised him and sent them to the vessel. He and his wife then joined the ship's company.

But once out on the ocean Sally became very seasick. The captain realized Sally's grave condition and headed for the nearest port, but Sally died two days later and was buried at sea. Quarll, left desolate, wished "ten thousand times" he had died with her. Becoming very melancholy, he refused to eat. The captain was afraid Quarll was going to die of grief, but eventually his interest in living came back.

Three weeks later they rounded Cape Horn. A period of calmness followed in which days went by without the ship moving more than a few miles. Reaching Acapulco, they sailed away with a fresh breeze, the wind north northeast. When the wind changed, they were pushed in close to rocky ledges near an island. Suddenly the main yard jammed. Quarll grabbed a hatchet and ran up the shrouds. Then came a terrific blast which shattered the ship on the rocky shore. Up astride of the main yard at the time, Philip was hurled through the air as if by a catapult to land on top of the rocks. One by one every other person aboard drowned.

Overcome by the sudden disaster, Quarll clambered to a comfortable plateau on the ledge where he pulled off his clothes, spread them in the sun, and fell into an exhausted sleep. Awakening several hours later, he looked around at the desolation. All he could see were dead bodies, broken planks, battered chests, and fragments of cargo.

Quarll went down as close as he could to the sea. Staring at the corpses he said, "Oh, that I was like one of you, past all dangers. I have shared with you in the terrors of death, why did I not also partake with you in its release? Why should I complain who have so much reason to be thankful? Had I been cut off when the cares of saving this worthless carcass stopped me from seeking the salvation of my soul, I should not have had the present opportunity of taking care of it."

Quarll climbed up on the rock and reached the top. There he discovered an opening through which he made his way. He now found himself in a beautiful meadow, beyond which he saw a lake, rolling plains, and tall trees.

"Heaven be praised," said he. "I shall not perish upon the barren rocks."

Reaching the lake and finding that the water was shallow, he took off his clothes and waded across with them in his arms. After dressing, Quarll walked for a distance, but he saw neither a human creature nor a habitation. In fact, after he walked all over the island in every direction, he found nothing but monkeys, strange beasts, and birds such as he had never seen before.

As he clambered down on the rocks again, he discovered a large codfish nearly six feet long in a pool where the late storm had cast it.

"Heaven be praised!" said he, "here is my dream right: where Providence rescued my life from the grim jaws of death, there it has provided me wherewithal to support it."

Stripping down, he climbed into the hole where the fish lay, pulled it out, and dragged it to higher ground. Quarll then found a number of oysters, mussels, and cockles which the sea had cast up along the rocky shore. Opening them with his knife, he ate a few.

Philip picked up a parcel of dry leaves, and with his knife and flint struck fire. Feeding it with twigs and then larger sticks, he soon had a good blaze. Over this fire Quarll broiled a slice of his fish, which he ate so heartily that it "overcame his stomach," being grown "weak with fasting." Having much "fatigued and harassed" himself in hauling the heavy fish up and down the rocks, he fell asleep, not awakening until the morning.

When dawn came he realized that he would have to build a house to protect himself from the weather. Having nothing but his knife, which could be of little service to him, Quarll decided to go to the rocks where he had been shipwrecked to see if he could find anything from the wreck that might be of use. With the branch of a tree to use as a staff, he walked over to the seashore. There he stripped himself and went into the water, groping along with his staff for sure footing, wading as high as his chin, diving to the bottom frequently, and feeling about with his hands. For almost two hours he searched, not daring to go out of his depth, but he did not find anything from the ship that could be used, not even a mast or any of the rigging.

He then recalled that when the ship struck he had a hatchet in his hand, and surmised that it probably was still on or near the rock where he was thrown. Reaching the ledge, he began to look around. He saw something like a handle just above the surface of the water at the base of the rock, and to his great joy, it proved to be the hatchet.

Carrying this precious tool, he went back to the valley, planning to cut down some trees to make himself a palisaded hut. Quarll found a type of tree whose branches were pliant, and cut a sufficient number of them to make his "barrack."

The next morning he walked out again to look for a pleasant and convenient place to build his hut. After hiking several hours, he could find none more sheltered from the cold winds than where he already slept, a location in the middle of the island. It was well fenced on the north and east sides with trees which stood very thick. Cutting down some trees that grew in his way, he cleared a spot of ground about twelve feet square, leaving one tree standing at each corner. With the young stalks he chopped down the day before, he filled the distance between, setting the tiny trees about six inches apart and leaving a larger vacancy for the door.

His frame house now being up, Quarll bent branches across from both sides for a roof, weaving them in and out. After he finished the top, he went about closing the sides, using large branches. He stripped off their small twigs and wove them between the plants "in the manner sheep-pens are made." Quarll constructed a door in the same fashion. By the time he finished all this work, half a month had gone by.

"Now," said he aloud, "here is a house, but where is the furniture? This, indeed, may keep the weather from me but not the cold. The ground on which I do and must lie, is hard, and doubtless in the winter will grow damp, which, with want of covering, may occasion agues and fevers, the cholic and the rheumatism, and twenty racking distempers, which may cause me to repent my having escaped a milder death."

One day he went to see if he could spy any ships within sight of the island. As he was walking along, "full of heavy and dull thoughts, which weighed his looks to the ground," he happened to find some high grass near a grove of trees which he had not seen before.

"Heaven be praised," he said, "I have found wherewithal to keep my poor body from the ground, whilst I am by Providence, doomed to remain here." He cut down a sufficient quantity of grass to weave into mats to serve him instead of bed and bedclothes. Eventually he finished his mats and was able to use them.

His next discovery was a tree root which when baked tasted like bread, "and that of a most delicious kind." He went across to dig a good quantity of the root, but as he was starting out he saw a large tortoise crawling before him.

"Heaven be praised!" said he, "here is what will supply me both with victuals, and a dish to cook it in." He ran and turned the tortoise on its back to keep it from getting away while he went to fetch his hatchet.

He killed and dressed the tortoise and "liked it extremely, some part of it eating very much like veal." This was a joy to him, for he had eaten no fresh meat for a long time. Having boiled it all, he laid by the remainder to eat now and then between his meals of fish, of which he had grown tired.

He used the tortoise shell from time to time as a cooking dish. He often varied his diet by means of the roots he had been so fortunate in discovering. Some he roasted for bread, others he boiled with salt cod.

After several trips around the island he estimated it to be eleven miles in circumference, of an oblong form, going "in and out" in several places. The south end was nearly twice "as broad as the opposite." No one, however, has ever identified on today's maps or charts the place where Quarll lived.

One day while hiking on the beach he found a chest filled with merchandise which had been washed up by a late storm. He went home, got his hatchet, and wrenched the chest open. He found a suit of clothes and some linen.

"These," said he, "neither the owner nor I want." He then took out a roll of several sheets of parchment which were blank. "These," said he, "I will make records of heaven's mercies, and Providence's wonderful liberality to me; so instead of being the ruin of some they may chance to be the reclaiming of others."

At the bottom of the chest lay a rundlet of brandy, a Cheshire cheese, a leather bottle full of ink, with a parcel of pens and a penknife. "As for these," said he, "they are of use; the pens, ink, and parchments have equipped me to keep a journal, which will divert and pass away a few anxious hours: as for the cheese and brandy, they will but cause me new cares: before I had them I wanted them not; now the benefit and comfort I shall find in them, when gone, will make me hanker after them; I wish I had still been without them; but now they are here, it would be a sin to let them be lost. I will take them home, and will only use them at my need; which will make them hold out the longer, and me grow less fond of them."

By degrees he took home the chest and its contents. Now having materials to begin his journal, he immediately fell to work writing the story of his life from the time he was eight years old to the day of his being cast away, the tenth of July, 1675, when he was twenty-eight years of age. He found the chest on the fifteenth of September, 1675.

The season now being fairly far advanced, he gathered a store of fuel and roots and began to line the outside of his barrack with a wall of turf, and lay the same at the top, to keep out the rain.

One day after spring had come, he visited the northeast side of the rock and discovered at the foot of the boulder an extraordinarily large whale which the last high wind had cast there. On measuring the length of it, he estimated it to be ninety feet long.

With his knife, which he always carried, he gouged several slices of blubber off the whale and threw them to the small fish, saying, "It is but just you should, at last, feed on that which so long fed on you." When oil ran in abundance from the place he had cut the slices, he was vexed to see it wasted. "But why," said he, "should I be disturbed at it? What use have I for any? Providence takes none, it gives me all gratis." He went on feeling for oysters with his staff. As the days went by, the whale meat gave him many delightful meals.

While investigating various roots one afternoon, he found several that looked edible. He snapped a bit off each one, and if they broke off short, were not stringy, and did not have a disagreeable scent, he tasted them. Some were sweetish, others sharp and hot, like horse-radish, and those he proposed to use instead of spice. "Sure," said he, "these being of a pleasant scent and flavor, cannot be of an offensive nature," and so he took a sample of every root which he judged edible, and boiled them as the surest way to experience their goodness.

One morning he saw a number of monkeys of two different tribes. One group was squealing and fighting against the other. He stood for some time admiring the order they kept, and the battle continued fiercely. He went closer to discover what they fought about, and found that the cause was a great field of wild pomegranates.

Later Quarll visited the field and took home some of the fruit. He ate several, after which he fell into a peculiar sleep, during which time he had a truly fantastic dream of such improbable nature that it has no place in this volume.

He reasoned that the monkeys must have been fighting over the pomegranates because of the unusual results of eating the fruit, and decided to omit the pomegranates from his diet in the immediate future.

He now promised God and heaven that he had been so pleased on the island that as he was content, he would never try to escape and return to civilization.

One day some months later a ship appeared off the island. Those aboard sighted Quarll high on the hill waving vigor-

ously; and putting a small boat over the side of the ship, the
sailors started rowing ashore. So excited was Philip that he
forgot all about his resolution to forsake civilization and
spend the rest of his days on the island. Suddenly, as the
sailors neared the island, the wind began to freshen so that
it was difficult to row the boat through the dangerous rocks.
They persisted in their rescue efforts for several hours, struggling against the increasing waves, but they finally were
forced to abandon their attempts when their craft struck
against a number of rocks in succession. Afraid that they
would either smash the boat or sink it, the sailors returned
to the ship without rescuing Quarll.

As he watched the ship sail away, Philip became very unhappy and cried out, "Whither shall I now fly for help? The
world can give me none and I dare not crave any more from
heaven."

Some time later he went down to view the sea, Philip
noticed on the shore a large wooden canoe made from
a hollow tree. This made him think of canoes which the Indians paddled up and down their rivers. The canoe being on
that side of the rock next to California,* he fancied at the
time that the Indians might have come out to visit the island.
Possibly, he reasoned, it was one of the Indians' canoes and
the owner might be on the island at that very moment. Con-
cealing himself, Quarll watched carefully for a chance to
hurry to the hut, but even then it was too late. When he tried
to get home to hide his valuables, he found visitors had already been there. His clothes, some very unusual shells, and
his bow and arrows were all missing. He ran out to the rock
again with his club, hoping to stop the intruders, but they
were already in the canoe, half a league from the rock.

As he watched their progress, he saw a great wave hit the
canoe, capsizing the two occupants and spilling everything

---

* The nearest mainland apparently was Mexico.

into the sea. The men drowned. While he was standing there Quarll was surprised to see two more men come down on the rocky ledge. Each took a bundle and went over to another boat concealed behind the rock, putting their load into it. With a long oar they pushed it offshore. They rowed the small boat out to the long boat, which had also been out of his view just behind another jutting section of the rock. Far in the distance was a ship at anchor. Philip realized that these "villains" had most sacrilegiously rifled and ransacked his habitation, not leaving even one of the mats to keep "his poor body warm" and off the ground.

After emptying their stolen goods into the long boat, the men returned to land and started for Philip's hut again. They took his winter garb and also seized what else they could find for their own use. Confronting the two men, Quarll discovered that they were French, and asked them if they would not leave him something on the island, but they refused. Everything they could move they took away.

The two men decided to tie him up and carry him away. They started for him, but when he grabbed his club, they kept their distance, wondering just how they could capture him. Backing slowly away, Quarll reached the forest, took to his heels and hid. Finally the strangers left the island, rowed out to their vessel and sailed away.

Worn out from the excitement, Quarll went into his house and decided to sleep. Although the invaders had stolen his bed, he was so tired that he went to sleep on the planking of the hut.

One day more than a year later the French mariners returned. This time they were determined to capture Quarll and take him away from his island. The invaders had ropes to bind him and guns to shot him. They brought saws and hatchets to cut down logwood and brazil, pickaxes and shovels to dig up roots, and flat-bottom boats to tow in shallow water. After rowing several loads out to their vessel, they returned and began filling two other flatboats. No sooner did they start their work than a storm arose, which increased in intensity and fury until their slender craft was dashed to pieces. Quarll watched as his tormentors sank into the sea and perished.

Back on shore, unseen by Philip, a French lad from the vessel was still alive. He had been loading material into one of the flatboats which was secured to a rock. The high waves which developed capsized his boat so that he was trapped under it. Later Quarll went out to see if he could find any debris from the storm and saw the overturned boat on the rocks. He walked toward it.

Suddenly he heard a voice cry out, a voice he thought was a woman's.

"Heaven be praised," said he, "there is somebody whom I have come to save, someone to be my companion, I cannot help but rejoice at the event." Hastening to the boat, he again heard the voice. "Certainly," said he, "this must be some woman from the sound." This fired his blood and set his heart beating. "Now," said he, "Providence has completed my happiness. I shall have a companion and helpmate."

Then came a cry in French, "For Christ's sake let me out."

Philip leaned over and struggled to raise the capsized flatboat. He jammed the end of his staff under the craft and lifted it up about a foot from the ground. The French boy crawled out, expecting Quarll to kill him. Quarll, who had until that moment believed there was a woman inside, overcame his disappointment. He ordered the boy to assist him so he could set the boat on its bottom, which was accomplished without much effort. The boy now fell on his knees and asked forgiveness for helping the other Frenchmen to rob him.

Quarll told the lad to help him pick up wreckage on the beach. Each of them took up what he could carry back to the hut. Instead of scolding him, Quarll was very gentle to the boy, and they reached the house comparatively good friends.

Quarll found that the youth was really industrious, although without question he had been a thief. From that day on, the lad was taught many things and developed into a fairly good companion for Quarll.

One afternoon, however, the boy vanished. He had gone down to the shore to get oysters to make sauce for some fresh codfish which Philip was dressing. It was possible that while there the boy had hailed a ship which had suddenly come into view, and her crew had picked him up.

Quarll later that day did see a ship leaving the island, but it was not until the boy failed to return that he began to get worried. At first he feared that the lad had met with trouble down on the rocks, but when he found the boy's bag of oysters and the rake, he decided the lad had sailed away on the ship. He never saw him again.

One day when Quarll returned to his hut he found a monkey which was an outstandingly beautiful creature of the red variety. The animal was friendly for some reason and surprisingly good-natured. Within a relatively short time Quarll had made a pet of it and named it "Beaufidelle." When in some strange way the monkey became jealous of a picture of a woman Philip had known, he took it down from the wall. Quarll and Beaufidelle soon became firm companions, and the monkey now followed him everywhere he went.

Then came a terrible morning when the other monkeys cornered Beaufidelle at the pomegranate field and gave him such a beating that they fatally wounded him. Philip found his pet and carried him home. Although the monkey lingered for a week, he finally died.

For the next four years nothing happened that Quarll mentions except great thunderstorms in the summer and an abundance of hail and snow in the winter. Sometimes fragments of ships and battered casks washed in around the rocks, and broken chests with planks and other similar debris came ashore from shipwrecks.

Philip now had several hours of idleness in the daytime, which with his late beloved Beaufidelle would have slipped away pleasurably. Now they dragged slowly on, loaded with dull and heavy thoughts that made his walks "irksome."

Finally came the day when Dorrington went ashore to visit Quarll and made such a favorable impression on the old man that he decided to give Dorrington the manuscripts and documents of his unusual Robinson Crusoe-like existence.

Back in Bristol, as the years went by, Dorrington often thought of the lonely inhabitant of the island paradise, but he never heard of him again in any way. Possibly Frenchmen, prompted by stories the boy gave them, returned to the island, but if they did, nothing is recorded of such a visit.

In the two centuries and more which have elapsed since Dorrington left the island, no further word has ever come back to the English-speaking world of the hermit Quarll.

THE MASSACRE

Early in the year 1802 a resident of Scituate, Massachusetts, John Dorthy by name, went to Boston where he signed on as one of the crew of the ship *Boston,* which was owned in Massachusetts by Messrs. Francis and Thomas Amory. In due time he sailed on the ship to Hull, England. Here an additional man joined the crew, and were it not for his presence, we would never have known what happened to Dorthy after he left England.*

The captain, John Salter, went ashore at Hull to buy a substantial amount of hardware for barter as well as to have minor repairs and alterations made on the *Boston.* His blacksmith work was done by a Mr. Jewitt whose son, John R. Jewitt, became a friend of Captain Salter. When young Jewitt learned of the long voyage the captain planned to take to the west coast of what is now Canada and then across to China, he was eager to go with him.

Salter suggested to John that he might become a member of the crew, if he wished. Although there was already a

* I would not have been given the details of the *Boston*'s voyage but for the kindness of Richard Rohe of Somerville, Massachusetts, whose ancestor bequeathed Rohe the original account.

blacksmith aboard, with the lad's knowledge of blacksmith work he could be the armorer and have a blacksmith's forge right on board. Young Jewitt decided to accept the offer and bade farewell to his family. On the third day of September, 1802, the *Boston* sailed from the Downs with fair winds in company with twenty-four American sailing vessels, most of which were bound home. Jewitt kept a careful record of the journey. Were it not for his journal the fate of the others in the crew would never have been known. The following are extracts from what he wrote:

⚓

    I was sea-sick for a few of the first days but it was of short continuance, and on my recovery I found myself in uncommonly fine health and spirits, and went to work with alacrity at my forge, in putting in order some of the muskets, and making daggers, knives, and small hatchets for the Indian trade, while in wet and stormy weather I was occupied below in filing and polishing them. This was my employment, having but little to do with sailing the vessel, though I used occasionally to lend a hand in assisting the seamen in taking in and making sail.

    As I had never before been out of sight of land, I cannot describe my sensations, after I had recovered from the distressing effects of seasickness, on viewing the mighty ocean by which I was surrounded, bounded only by the sky; while its waves rising in mountains, seemed every moment to threaten our ruin.

    We had a pleasant and favorable passage of twenty-nine days to the Island of St. Catharine on the coast of Brazil, where the Captain had determined to stop for a few days to obtain wood and water. This place belongs to the Portuguese.

On entering the harbor we were saluted by the fort which we returned. The next day the Governor of the Island came on board of us with his suite: Captain Salter received him with much respect and invited him to dine with him, which he accepted.

The ship remained at St. Catharine's four days, during which time we were busily employed in taking in wood, water, and fresh provisions, Captain Salter thinking it best to furnish himself here with a full supply for his voyage to the North West coast, so as not to be obliged to stop at the Sandwich Islands. St. Catharine is a very commodious place for vessels to stop at that are bound round Cape Horn, as it abounds with springs of fine water, with excellent oranges, plantains, and bananas.

Having completed our stores we put to sea, and on the twenty-fifth of December at length passed Cape Horn, which we had made no less than thirty-six days before, but were repeatedly forced back by contrary winds, experiencing very rough and tempestuous weather in doubling it.

Immediately after passing Cape Horn, all our dangers and difficulties seemed to be at an end; the weather became fine and so little labour was necessary on board the ship that the men soon recovered from their fatigue and were in excellent spirits. A few days after, we fell in with an English South Sea Whaling Ship, homeward bound, which was the only vessel we spoke with on our voyage. We now took the trade wind or monsoon, during which we enjoyed the finest weather possible, so that for the space of a fortnight we were not obliged to reeve a topsail or to make a tack, and so light was the duty and easy the life of the sailors during this time, that they appeared the happiest of any people in the world.

Captain Salter, who had been for many years in the East India trade, was a most excellent seaman, and preserved the strictest order and discipline on board his ship, though he was a man of mild temper and conciliating manners, and disposed to allow every indulgence to his men, not inconsistent with their duty.

We had on board a fine band of music, with which on Saturday nights, when the weather was pleasant, we were accustomed to be regaled, the Captain ordering them to play for several hours for the amusement of the crew. This to me was most delightful, especially during the serene evenings we experienced in traversing the Southern Ocean. As for myself, during the day I was constantly occupied at my forge, in re-fitting or repairing some of the iron work of the vessel, but principally in making tomahawks, daggers, &c. for the North West coast.

In this manner, with a fair wind and easy weather from the 28th of December, the period of our passing Cape Horn, we pursued our voyage to the Northward until the 12th of March, 1803, when we made Woody Point in Nootka Sound on the North West Coast of America. We immediately stood up the Sound for Nootka, where Captain Salter had determined to stop, in order to supply the ship with wood and water before proceeding up the coast to trade.

But in order to avoid the risque of any molestation or interruption to his men from the Indians, while thus employed, he proceeded with the ship about five miles to the Northward of the village, which is situated on Friendly Cove and sent out his chief mate with several of the crew in the boat to find a good place for anchoring her.

After sounding for some time they returned with information that they had discovered a secure place for anchorage, on the Western side of an inlet or small bay at about half a mile from the coast, near a small island which protected it from the sea, and where there was plenty of wood and excellent water. This ship accordingly came to anchor in this place, at twelve o'clock at night, in twelve fathom water, muddy bottom, and so near the shore that to prevent the ship from winding we secured her by a hawser to the trees.

On the morning of the next day, the thirteenth, several of the natives came on board in a canoe from the village of Nootka, with their king, called Maquina, who appeared much pleased on seeing us, and with great seeming cordiality welcomed Capt. Salter and his officers to his country. As I had never before beheld a savage of any nation, it may readily be supposed that the novelty of their appearance, so different from any people that I had hitherto seen, excited in me strong feelings of surprise and curiosity.

I was, however, particularly struck with the looks of their king, who was a man of a dignified aspect, about six feet in height and extremely strait and well proportioned; his features were in general good and his face was rendered remarkable by a large Roman nose, a very uncommon form of feature among these people; his complexion was of a dark copper hue, though his face, legs, and arms were on this occasion, so covered with red paint, that their natural colour could scarcely be perceived, his eye-brows were painted black in two broad stripes like a new moon, and his long black hair, which shone with oil, was fastened in a bunch on the top of his head and strewed or powdered all over with white down, which gave him a most curious and extraordinary appearance.

He was dressed in a large mantle or cloak of the black sea otter skin, which reached to his knees, and was fastened around his middle by a broad belt of the cloth of the country, wrought, or painted with figures of several colours; this dress was by no means unbecoming, but on the contrary had an air of savage magnificence.

His men were habited in mantles of the same cloth, which is made from the bark of a tree, and has some resemblance to straw matting; these are nearly square and have two holes in the upper part large enough to admit the arms.

↩

The natives began to come aboard in increasing numbers, some to bring salmon, others apparently to watch young Jewitt at the forge. By March 20, the *Boston* had taken aboard sufficient wood and water and was nearly ready for departure.

The next day Maquina and Captain Salter had a serious argument concerning a gun, following which the chief went ashore visibly upset.

On March 22 Maquina again came aboard with many Indians to ask the captain when he planned to sail. Captain Salter replied that they were leaving the next day. Maquina then invited Salter to go fishing for salmon with him as the fresh fish would come in handy. After some discussion it was decided to put part of the crew ashore that afternoon to fish, while Maquina and his chiefs would remain on board with the others.

Shortly after the departure of the boats John Jewitt went down to his bench in the steerage where he was employed in cleaning muskets. He had not been there more than an hour when he heard the men hoisting in the longboat, which, a few minutes later, "was succeeded by a great bustle and confusion on deck. His chronicle continues:

⚓

I immediately ran up the steerage stairs, but scarcely was my head above deck, when I was caught by the hair by one of the savages, and lifted from my feet; fortunately for me my hair being short, and the ribbon with which it was tied slipping, I fell from his hold into the steerage. As I was falling, he struck at me with an axe, which cut a deep gash in my forehead, and penetrated the skull, but in consequence of his losing his hold, I luckily escaped the full force of the blow; which, otherwise, would have cleft my head in two.

I fell, stunned and senseless upon the floor—how long I continued in this situation I know not, but on recovering my senses the first thing that I did, was to try to get up; but so weak was I, from the loss of blood, that I fainted and fell. I was however soon recalled to my recollection by three loud shouts or yells from the savages, which convinced me that they had got possession of the ship. It is impossible for me to describe my feelings at this terrific sound. Some faint idea may be formed of them by those who had known what it is to half waken from a hideous dream and still think it real.

Never, no, never, shall I lose from my mind, the impression of that dreadful moment. I expected every instant to share the wretched fate of my unfortunate companions, and when I heard the song of triumph, by which these infernal yells was succeeded, my blood ran cold in my veins.

Having at length sufficiently recovered my senses to look around me after wiping the blood from my eyes, I saw that the hatch of the steerage was shut. This was done, as I afterwards discovered, by order of Maquina, who, on seeing the savage strike at me with the axe, told him not to hurt me, for that I was the armourer, and would be useful to them in repairing their arms; while at the same time to prevent any of his men from injuring me, he had the hatch closed.

But to me this circumstance wore a very different appearance, for I thought that those barbarians had only prolonged my life in order to deprive me of it by the most

cruel tortures. I remained in this horrid state of suspense
for a very long time, when at length the hatch was opened,
and Maquina, calling me by name, ordered me to come up.
I groped my way up as well as I was able, being almost
blinded with the blood that flowed from my wound, and so
weak as with difficulty to walk. The king, on perceiving my
situation, ordered one of his men to bring a pot of water to
wash the blood from my face, which having done, I was able
to see distinctly with one of my eyes, but the other was so
swollen from my wound, that it was closed.

But what a terrific spectacle met my eyes; six naked savages, standing in a circle around me, covered with the blood
of my murdered comrades, with their daggers uplifted in
their hands, prepared to strike. I now thought my last moment had come and recommended my soul to my Maker.—

The king, who, as I have already observed, knew enough
of English to make himself understood, entered the circle,
and placing himself before me, addressed me nearly in the
following words—"John—I speak—you no say no—You say
no—daggers come!" He then asked me if I would be his slave
during my life—If I would fight for him in his battles—If I
would repair his muskets and make daggers and knives for
him—with several other questions, to all of which I was careful to answer, yes. He then told me that he would spare my
life, and ordered me to kiss his hands and feet to show my
submission to him, which I did—

In the mean time his people were very clamorous to have
me put to death, so that there should be none of us left to
tell our story to our countrymen and prevent them from coming to trade with them; but the king, in the most determined
manner opposed their wishes, and to his favour am I wholly
indebted for my being yet among the living.

As I was busy at work at the time of the attack, I was without my coat, and what with the coldness of the weather, my

feebleness from loss of blood, the pain of my wound and the extreme agitation and terror that I still felt, I shook like a leaf, which the king observing, went into the cabin and bringing up a great coat that belonged to the Captain, threw it over my shoulders, telling me to drink some rum from a bottle which he handed me at the same time, giving me to understand that it would be good for me and keep me from trembling as I did. I took a draught of it, after which, taking me by the hand, he led me to the quarter deck, where the most horrid sight presented itself that ever my eyes witnessed —the heads of our unfortunate Captain and his crew, to the number of twenty-five, were all arranged in a line, and Maquina ordering one of his people to bring a head, asked me whose it was: I answered, the Captain's; in like manner the others were shewed me, and I told him the names, excepting a few that were so horribly mangled that I was not able to recognize them.

I now discovered that all our unfortunate crew had been massacred, and learned that after getting possession of the ship, the savages had broke open the arms chest and magazine, and supplying themselves with ammunition and arms, sent a party on shore to attack our men who had gone thither to fish, and being joined by numbers from the village, without difficulty overpowered and murdered them, and cutting off their heads, brought them on board, after throwing their bodies into the sea.

On looking upon the deck, I saw it entirely covered with the blood of my poor comrades, whose throats had been cut with their own jack-knives, the savages having seized the opportunity while they were busy in hoisting in the boat to grapple with them and overpower them by their numbers; in the scuffle the Captain was thrown overboard and dispatched by those in the canoes who immediately cut off his head: What I felt on this occasion, may be more readily conceived than expressed.

After I had answered his questions, Maquina took my silk handkerchief from my neck and bound it around my head, placing over the wound a leaf of tobacco, of which we had a quantity on board. This was done at my desire, as I had often found from personal experience the benefit of this application to cuts.

Maquina then ordered me to get the ship under weigh for Friendly Cove. This I did by cutting the cables and sending some of the natives aloft to loose the sails, which they performed in a very bungling manner. But they succeeded so far in loosing the jib and topsails, that, with the advantage of a fair wind, I succeeded in getting the ship into the Cove, where, by order of the king, I ran her ashore on a sandy beach, at 8 o'clock at night.

The inhabitants in great excitement all gathered at the shore. Maquina escorted John Jewitt to the chief's house where five hundred warriors began to assemble. Here Jewitt quickly made friends with the king's eleven-year-old son, Sat-sat-sak-sis, by cutting off the metal buttons from his coat and tying them around the boy's neck like a necklace. Jewitt was now told to sleep in the quarters which the lad occupied, as Maquina feared several of the natives would kill John before morning.

When he learned at midnight that sailmaker John Thompson had been discovered on board the *Boston* still alive, Jewitt decided to pretend that Thompson, who was forty, was his father. In this way he might influence Maquina to keep Thompson alive.

When morning came, Maquina told Jewitt that he was

going to kill Thompson and ordered John and the eleven-year-old prince to go with him. Maquina within an hour had all the tribe assembled on the beach. Before the meeting began, John asked Maquina if he loved his son. Maquina agreed. John then asked the lad if he loved his father, and the boy answered in the affirmative.

"I also love my father," John cried out, "and I believe he is the one still alive on board."

John threw himself on his knees at Maquina's feet, imploring the king to spare his father's life. "If you kill my father, kill me also," John cried out.

Maquina then decided to let John go on board, and if it were his father who was still alive, to bring him ashore.

John went on board to find that Thompson was wounded, but not seriously, and had been hiding in the hold. He had scuffled with an Indian who had discovered him.

John cautioned Thompson to go along with the father story and Thompson agreed. In this manner the second white man was gradually accepted by the tribe.

As the days went by, the natives stripped the ship, cutting away the spars and masts, and carrying all stores to the king's house. While rummaging in the cabin, John found several blank account books and the captain's writing desk which he took ashore with the permission of the chief.

Several weeks later, two other craft, the ships *Mary* and *Juno* of Boston, Massachusetts, appeared off shore. The Indians began to shoot at the ships which replied with cannon fire. After sending a few cannonballs ashore, the two craft wore * ship and stood out to sea.

A short time later one of the savages went on board the *Boston* with a firebrand to explore in the hold. By mistake

* To wear ship is to put a vessel on the other tack by bringing the craft round stern to wind. It is the opposite to tacking, which is bringing her head to the wind, or to "go about."

he set the ship afire. She was destroyed by the flames, which consumed most of the cargo still on board.

During the middle of April there occurred an incident in which John Thompson almost lost his life. A native ran to Jewitt and told him that the king was about to shoot his father. Jewitt rushed over to the king's residence where he found the enraged Maquina holding a gun to Thompson's head. Slipping up to Maquina, John begged him not to shoot. Maquina finally calmed down.

It developed that Thompson had struck Prince Sat-sat-sak-sis because the lad was teasing him. Many weeks went by before Maquina would even speak to Thompson, who apparently was undiplomatic and always in trouble.

The time came when Maquina suggested that Jewitt should marry, but John steadfastly refused. Finally Maquina said that his white slave would have to choose a woman for himself. After much objection from John, Maquina took the reluctant Jewitt to another tribe so that John would have more choice. John finally picked out a girl of seventeen as his bride.

A wedding ceremony followed during which John discovered that his bride's name was Eu-stoch-ee-exqua. They lived together for a time, but when Maquina found they were not happy, he allowed them to separate.

On January 15, 1805, an eclipse of the moon terrified the natives, who did not lose their fear until the phenomenon had ended. John then attempted to explain the eclipse, but the natives did not believe him. They actually expected that the earth would be swallowed up.

On various occasions John had written letters pleading for rescue to be delivered to captains of ships trading along the coast. One day he met the king of the Wickinninish tribe who wanted to purchase John from Maquina. Although Maquina refused, John was able surreptitiously to give the

Wickinninish chief a letter to be delivered to "any ship's captain." This letter actually was turned over to the master of a brig some time later, and because of it the presence of John Jewitt and John Thompson at Nootka became known to the captains of almost every sailing craft in the general area.

The months went by, and with their passing John's hope for early freedom began to wane. There had been reports of seven different vessels on the coast, but not one came to Nootka. Probably the massacre on the *Boston*, the largest, strongest, and best equipped of any craft ever fitted out for the northwest trade, had given the commanders of other ships a general dread of the area.

In the letter which John had written imploring other white men to come "to the relief of two unfortunate Christians who were suffering among heathen," John told about the *Boston*'s capture and explained that there was not the least danger in a ship's coming to Nootka providing they would follow careful directions, which he gave in detail.

Then, on July 19, without any previous warning, John's ears were "saluted with the joyful sound of three cannon," and the cries of the inhabitants, exclaiming, "Wenna, weena —Mamethlee," that is, "Strangers—white men." At the time Jewitt was forging daggers for the king with Thompson's help.

Several of the natives came running into the house, to tell John that a vessel under full sail was coming into the harbor. "Though my heart bounded with joy, I repressed my feelings, and affecting to pay no attention to what was said I told Thompson to be on his guard, and not betray any joy, as our release, and perhaps our lives, depended on our conducting ourselves so as to induce the natives to suppose we were not very anxious to leave them."

They continued working as if nothing had happened. A

few minutes later Maquina came in. Seeing John at work, he appeared much surprised and asked him if he did not know that a vessel had come. John answered in a careless manner, saying that it was nothing to him.

"How, John," said Maquina, "you no glad go board?" John replied that he cared very little about it, as he had become reconciled to the Indian manner of living and had no wish to go away. Maquina then told John that he had called a council of his people about John and Thompson and that they must be present at the meeting.

When all the men had gathered at Maquina's house, he asked them what should be done with Thompson and John now that a vessel had arrived. Should he go on board himself to make a trade and procure such articles as were wanted?

Almost every man gave his opinion: some were for putting the white men to death; others, less barbarous, were for sending John and Thompson back into the country until the vessel sailed.

Toowinnakinnish, a young man of twenty-three, the only son of Toopeeshottee who was the oldest and most respected chief of the tribe, voted for the release of the two men. Toowinnakinnish had always been remarkably kind and friendly to John, and John had in return frequently made special daggers and knives for the young man, who was one of the handsomest men among them. Very amiable, and much milder in his manners than any of the others, Toowinnakinnish was neater both in his person and in the way he ran his house.

Almost every man voted against Maquina's going on board the vessel. They feared that the captain of the ship would kill him or keep him a prisoner in consequence of his having destroyed the *Boston*. When Maquina had heard their opinions, he told them he was not afraid of being hurt but that he

would be guided by John, whom he had always found to be
a truthful man.

Maquina then turned to John and asked him if he thought
there would be any danger in his going on board. Jewitt
answered that while he was not surprised at what the people
said, he had no reason to believe that the whites would attempt to harm the king.

After reflecting a few moments, Maquina asked John to
write a letter to the captain telling him that he had treated
Thompson and John kindly since they had been with him.

Inwardly elated, but keeping his feelings well under control, John explained to Maquina he was indifferent about
writing the letter but would do it if Maquina really
wished. Jewitt now set about composing a letter which could
determine his future life.

John hoped that he would not be condemned for making
use of "an occasion which afforded me the only hope of ever
more beholding a Christian country, and preserving myself,
if not from death, at least from a life of continued suffering."
As he knew neither the name of the captain or the brig, he
wrote as follows:

To Captain _____,

of the Brig _____,

Nootka, July 19, 1805

Sir,

The bearer of this letter is the Indian king by the
name of Maquina. He was the instigator of the capture of
the ship *Boston*, of Boston in North America, John Salter
captain, and of the murder of twenty-five men of her crew,
the two only survivors being now on shore—Wherefore I
hope you will take care to confine him according to his
merits, putting in your dead lights,* and keeping so good a

___

* Deadlights are strong shutters fixed outside a porthole or gunport to
keep out water in a storm. In this case they kept Maquina from escaping.

watch over him, that he cannot escape from you. By so doing
we shall be able to obtain our release in the course of a few
hours.

JOHN R. JEWITT, Armourer
of the *Boston,* for himself and
John Thompson, Sail-maker of said ship

John was later asked how he dared to write in this manner.
From long residence among these people, he explained, he
knew that he had little to worry about from their anger on
hearing that their king was confined if they knew his life depended upon John's release. They would sooner have given
up five hundred white men than have him injured.

His account continues:

On my giving the letter to Maquina, he asked me to explain it to him. This I did line by line, as he pointed them
out with his finger, but in a sense very different from the
real, giving him to understand that I had written to the captain, that as he had been kind to me since I had been taken
by him, that it was my wish that the captain should treat him
accordingly, and give him what molasses, biscuit, and rum
he wanted.

When I had finished, placing his finger in a significant
manner on my name at the bottom, and eyeing me with a
look that seemed to read my inmost thoughts, he said to me,
"John, you no lie?" Never did I undergo such a scrutiny, or
ever experience greater apprehensions than I felt at that
moment, when my destiny was suspended on the slightest
thread, and the least mark of embarrassment on mine, or
suspicion of treachery on his part, would probably have rendered my life the sacrifice.

Fortunately I was able to preserve my composure, and my

being painted in the Indian manner, which Maquina had since my marriage, required of me, prevented any change in my countenance from being noticed, and I replied with considerable promptitude, looking at him in my turn, with all the confidence I could muster, "Why do you ask me such a question, Tyee; have you ever known me to lie?"

"No."

"Then how can you suppose I should tell you a lie now, since I have never done it?" As I was speaking, he still continued looking at me with the same piercing eye, but observing nothing to excite his suspicion, he told me that he believed what I said was true, and that he would go on board, and gave orders to get ready his canoe.

His chiefs again attempted to dissuade him, using every argument for that purpose, while his wives crowded around him, begging him on their knees, not to trust himself with the white men. Fortunately for my companion and myself, so strong was his wish of going on board the vessel, that he was deaf to their solicitations, and making no other reply to them, than, "John no lie," he left the house, taking four prime skins with him as a present to the captain.

Scarcely had the canoe left the shore when Maquina ordered his men to stop. Calling to John, he asked him if he did not want to go on board. John craftily replied that he had no wish to go, not having any desire to leave his friends.

As soon as he went on board the brig *Lydia*, Maquina gave his present of skins and John's letter to the captain. On reading it, Captain Hill asked him into the cabin where he gave him some biscuit and a glass of rum. At the same time the captain privately directed his mate to go forward and return with five or six of the armed men.

As Jewitt tells the tale:

⚓

When they appeared, Captain Hill told Maquina that
he was his prisoner. Until the two men, whom he knew to be
on shore were released, Maquina was to be confined. The
captain ordered him to be put in irons, and the windows secured, which was instantly done, and two men placed as a
guard over him. Maquina was greatly surprised, actually terrified, at this reception. However, he made no attempt to
resist but requested the captain to permit one of his men to
come and see him.

One of them was accordingly called, and Maquina said
something to him which the captain did not understand, but
supposed to be an order to release us, when the man returning to his canoe, it was paddled off with the utmost expedition to the shore. As the canoe approached, the inhabitants,
who had all collected on the beach, manifested some uneasi-
ness at not seeing their king on board, but when on its
arrival, they were told that the captain had made him a prisoner, and that John had spoke bad about him in the letter,
they all both men and women, set up a loud howl, and ran
backwards and forwards upon the shore like so many lunatics,
scratching their faces, and tearing their hair in handfuls from
their heads.

After they had beat about in this manner for some time,
the men ran to their huts for their weapons, as if preparing
to attack an invading enemy; Maquina's wives and the rest
of the women, came around me, and throwing themselves on
their knees, begged me with tears to spare his life. Sat-sat-
sak-sis, who kept constantly with me, taking me by the hand,
wept bitterly, and joined his entreaties to theirs, that I would
not let the white men kill his father. I told them not to

afflict themselves, that Maquina's life was in no danger, nor would the least harm be done to him.

The men were, however, extremely exasperated with me, more particularly the common people, who came running in the most furious manner towards me, brandishing their weapons, and threatening to cut me in pieces no bigger than their thumb nails, while others declared they would burn me alive over a slow fire, suspended by the heels. All this fury, however, caused me but little alarm, as I felt convinced they would not dare to execute their hostages while the king was on board the brig.

The chiefs took no part in this violent conduct, but came to me, and enquired the reason why Maquina had been thus treated, and if the captain intended to kill him. I told them that if they would silence the people, so that I could be heard, I would explain all to them. They immediately put a stop to the noise, when I informed them that the captain in confining Maquina, had done it of his own accord, and only in order to make them release Thompson and myself, as he well knew we were with them, and if they would do that, their king would receive no injury, but be well treated, otherwise he would be kept a prisoner.

As many of them did not appear to be satisfied with this, and began to repeat their murderous threats—"Kill me," I said to them, "if it is your wish," throwing open the bear skin which I wore. "Here is my breast, I am only one among so many, and can make no resistance, but unless you wish to see your king hanging by his neck to that pole," pointing to the yard arm of the brig, "and the sailors firing at him with bullets, you will not do it."

I told them that their best plan would be to send Thompson on board, to desire the captain to use Maquina well till I was released, which would be soon. This they were perfectly willing to do, and I directed Thompson to go on board. But he objected, saying that he would not leave me alone with the savages. I told him not to be under any fear for me, for that if I could get him off, I could manage well enough for myself, and that I wished him immediately on getting on board the brig, to see the captain and request him to keep Maquina close till I was released, as I was in no danger while he had him safe.

When I saw Thompson off, I asked the natives what they intended to do with me. They said I must talk to the captain again, in another letter, and tell him to let his boat come on shore with Maquina, and that I should be ready to jump into the boat at the same time Maquina should jump on shore. I told them that the captain, who knew that they had killed my shipmates, would never trust his men so near the shore for fear they would kill them too, as they were so much more numerous, but that if they would select any three of their number to go with me in a canoe, when we came within hail, I could desire the captain to send his boat with Maquina, to receive me in exchange for him.

As I was going into the canoe, little Sat-sat-sak-sis, who could not bear to part with me, asked me, with an affecting simplicity, since I was going away to leave him, if the white men would let his father come on shore, and not kill him. I told him not to be concerned, for that no one should injure his father, when taking an affectionate leave of me, and again begging me not to let the white men hurt his father, he ran to comfort his mother, who was at a little distance, with the assurances I had given him.

On entering the canoe, I seated myself in the prow facing the three men, having determined if it was practicable, from the moment I found Maquina was secured, to get on board the vessel before he was released, hoping by that means to be enabled to obtain the restoration of what property belonging to the *Boston* still remained in the possession of the savages,

which I thought if it could be done, a duty that I owed to
the owners.

With feelings of joy impossible to be described, did I quit
this savage shore, confident now that nothing could thwart
my escape, or prevent the execution of the plan I had
formed, as the men appointed to convey and guard me were
armed with nothing but their paddles. As we came within
hail of the brig, they at once ceased paddling, when present-
ing my pistols at them, I ordered then instantly to go on, or
I would shoot the whole of them.

A proceeding so wholly unexpected, threw them into great
consternation, and resuming their paddles, in a few moments
to my inexpressible delight, I once more found myself along
side of a Christian ship, a happiness which I had almost despaired of ever again enjoying. All the crew crowded to the
side to see me, as the canoe came up, and manifested much
joy at my safety. I immediately leaped on board, where I was
welcomed by the Captain, Samuel Hill, of the brig *Lydia*
of Boston, who congratulated me on my escape informing me
that he had received my letter off Kla-iz-zart, from the chief
Mackee Ulatilla, who came off himself in his canoe, to deliver
it to him, on which he immediately proceeded hither to aid
me.

I returned him my thanks in the best manner I could for
his humanity, though I hardly knew what I said, such was
the agitated state of my feelings at that moment, with joy for
my escape, thankfulness to the Supreme Being who had so
mercifully preserved me, and gratitude to those whom he
had rendered instrumental in my delivery, that I have no
doubt, that what with my strange dress, being painted with
red and black from head to foot, having a bear skin wrapped
around me, and my long hair, which I was not allowed to cut,
fastened on the top of my head in a large bunch, with a sprig
of green spruce. I must have appeared more like one de-

ranged than a rational creature, as Captain Hill afterwards
told me, that he never saw any thing in the form of man, look
so wild as I did when I first came on board.

The Captain then asked me into the cabin, where I found
Maquina in irons, with a guard over him. He looked very
melancholy, but on seeing me his countenance brightened
up, and he expressed his pleasure with the welcome of
"Wocash John"; when taking him by the hand, I asked the
Captain's permission to take off his irons, assuring him that
as I was with him, there was no danger of his being in the
least troublesome.

He accordingly consented, and I felt a sincere pleasure in
freeing from fetters, a man, who, though he had caused the
death of my poor comrades, had nevertheless, always proved
my friend and protector, and whom I had requested to be
thus treated, only with a view of securing my liberty. Maquina smiled and appeared much pleased at this mark of
attention from me. When I had freed the king from his
irons, Captain Hill wished to learn the particulars of our
capture, observing that an account of the destruction of the
ship and her crew had been received at Boston before he
sailed, but that nothing more was known, except that two of
the men were living, for whose rescue the owners had offered
a liberal reward, and that he had been able to get nothing
out of the old man, whom the sailors had supplied so plenti-
fully with grog, as to bring him too much by the head to
give any information.

The Captain appeared to be convinced from what I said,
of the impolicy of taking Maquina's life, and said that he
would leave it wholly with me whether to spare or kill him,
as he resolved to incur no censure in either case. I replied
that I most certainly should never take the life of a man
who had preserved mine, had I no other reason, but as there
was some of the *Boston*'s property still remaining on shore,

I considered it a duty that I owed to those who were interested in that ship, to try to save it for them, and with that view I thought it would be well to keep him on board till it was given up. He concurred in this proposal, saying if there was any of the property left, it most certainly ought to be got.

During this conversation Maquina was in great anxiety, as from what English he knew he perfectly comprehended the subject of our deliberation; constantly interrupting me to enquire what we had determined to do with him, what the Captain said, if his life would be spared, and if I did not think that Thompson would kill him. I pacified him as well as I was able, by telling him that he had nothing to fear from the Captain, that he would not be hurt, and that if Thompson wished to kill him which was very probable, he would not be allowed to do it.

He would then remind me that I was indebted to him for my life, and that I ought to do by him, as he had done by me. I assured him that such was my intention, and I requested him to remain quiet, and not alarm himself, as no harm was intended him. But I found it extremely difficult to convince him of this, as it accorded so little with the ideas of revenge entertained by them. I told him however, that he must restore all the property still in his possession, belonging to the ship. This he was perfectly ready to do, happy to escape on such terms.

But as it was now past five, and too late for the articles to be collected, and brought off, I told him that he must content himself to remain on board with me that night, and in the morning he should be set on shore as soon as the things were delivered. To this he agreed, on condition that I would remain with him in the cabin. I then went upon deck, and the canoe that brought me having been sent back, I hailed the inhabitants, and told them that their king had agreed to stay on board till the next day, when he would return, but that no canoes must attempt to come near the vessel during the night, as they would be fired upon. They answered, "Woho, woho"—very well, very well.

I then returned to Maquina, but so great were his terrors, that he would not allow me to sleep, constantly disturbing me with his questions, and repeating, "John, you know when you was alone, and more than 500 men were your enemies, I was your friend, and prevented them from putting you and Thompson to death, and now I am in the power of your friends, you ought to do the same by me." I assured him that he would be detained on board no longer than the property was released, and that as soon as it was done, he would be set at liberty.

My pleasure was greatly damped by an unfortunate accident that occurred to Toowinnakinnish. That interesting young chief had come on board in the first canoe in the morning, anxious to see and comfort his king. He was received with much kindness by Captain Hill, from the favourable account I gave of him, and invited to remain on board.

As the muskets were delivered, he was in the cabin with Maquina, where was also the Captain, who on receiving them, snapped a number in order to try the locks; unluckily one of them happened to be loaded with swan shot, and going off, discharged its contents into the body of poor Toowinnakinnish, who was sitting opposite.

On hearing the report, I instantly ran into the cabin, where I found him weltering in his blood, with the Captain who was greatly shocked at the accident, endeavouring to assist him. We raised him up, and did every thing in our power to aid and comfort him, telling him that we felt much grieved at his misfortune, and that it was wholly unintentional. This he told me he was perfectly satisfied of, and while we dressed and bound up his wounds in the best manner we could, he bore the pain with great calmness, and bidding me farewell, was put on board one of the canoes, and taken on shore, where after languishing a few days, he expired. To me, his misfortune was a source of much affliction, as he had no share in the massacre of our crew, was of a most amiable character, and had always treated me with the greatest kindness and hospitality.

[In return for the cargo stolen from the *Boston,* their king was finally released to his tribe. Jewitt's narrative continues.]

The brig being under weigh, immediately on Maquina's quitting us, we proceeded to the northward, constantly keeping the shore in sight, and touching at various places for the purpose of trading.

Having already exceeded the bounds I had prescribed myself, I shall not attempt any account of our voyage upon the coast, or a description of the various nations we met with in the course of it, among whom were a people of a very singular appearance, called by the sailors the *Wooden-lips.* They have many skins, and the trade is principally managed by their women, who are not only expert in making a bargain, but are as dexterous in the management of their canoes, as the men are elsewhere.

After a period of nearly four months from our leaving Nootka, we returned from the northward to Columbia river, for the purpose of procuring masts, &c. for our brig, which had suffered considerably in her spars during a gale of wind.

We proceeded about ten miles up the river, to a small Indian village, where we heard from the inhabitants that Captains Clark and Lewis, from the United States of America, had been there about a fortnight before, on their journey over-land, and had left several medals with them, which they shewed us. The river at this place is of considerable breadth, and both sides of it from its entrance, covered with forests of the very fine pine timber, fir, and spruce, interspersed with Indian settlements.

Here after providing ourselves with spars, we sailed for Nootka, where we arrived in the latter part of November. The tribe being absent, the agreed signal was given, by firing a cannon, and in a few hours after a canoe appeared, which landed at the village, and putting the king * on shore, came off to the brig.

Enquiry was immediately made by Kinneclimmits, who was one of the three men in the canoe, if John was there, as the king had some skins to sell them if he was. I then went forward and invited them on board, with which they readily complied, telling me that Maquina had a number of skins with him, but that he would not come on board unless I would go on shore for him.

This I agreed to provided they would remain in the brig in the meantime. To this they consented, and the Captain taking them into the cabin, treated them with bread and molasses. I then went on shore in the canoe, notwithstanding the remonstrances of Thompson and the Captain, who, though he wanted the skins, advised me by no means to put myself in Maquina's power; but I assured him that I had no fear as long as those men were on board.

As I landed Maquina came up and welcomed me with much joy; on enquiring for the men, I told him that they were to remain until my return.

"Ah, John," said he, "I see you are afraid to trust me, but if they had come with you, I should not have hurt you, though I should have taken good care not to let you go on board of another vessel." He then took his chest of skins, and stepping into the canoe, I paddled him along-side the brig, where he was received and treated by Capt. Hill with the greatest cordiality, who bought of him his skins.

* Maquina had been hunting away from Nootka.

He left us much pleased with his reception, enquiring of me how many moons it would be before I should come back again to see him and his son, who had begged him hard to let him come with him to see me: saying, that he would keep all his furs for me, and that as soon as my son, who was then about five months old, was of a suitable age to take from his mother, he would send for him, and take care of him as his own.

As soon as Maquina had quitted us, we got under weigh, and stood again to the northward. We continued on the coast until the eleventh of August, 1806, when having completed our trade, we sailed for China, to the great joy of all our crew, and particularly so to me. With a degree of satisfaction that I can ill express, did I quit a coast to which I was resolved nothing should again tempt me to return, and as the tops of the mountain sunk in the blue waves of ocean, I seemed to feel my heart lightened of an oppressive load.

We left China in February, 1807, and after a pleasant voyage of 114 days, arrived at Boston. My feelings on once more finding myself in a Christian country, among a people speaking the same language with myself, may be more readily conceived than expressed. In the Post Office in that place, I found a letter for me from my mother, acknowledging the receipt of mine from China, expressing the great joy of my family on hearing of my being alive and well, whom they had for a long time given up for dead, and requesting me to write to them on receiving her letter, which I accordingly did.

While in Boston, I was treated with much kindness and hospitality by the owners of the ship *Boston*, Messrs. Francis and Thomas Amory of that place, to whom I feel myself under great obligations for their goodness to me, and the assistance which they so readily afforded a stranger in distress.

⟵

John Jewitt had with him several journals, together with
sketches which had been made by Second Mate William
Ingraham of New York while he was aboard the *Boston*.
He turned the material over to Judge Thomas Dawes of
Boston who had it delivered to Ingraham's family in New
York.

Details of John Jewitt's next few years are lacking, but
we do know that he resided in Middleton, Connecticut, in
the year 1815. At the time, he recorded, sailmaker John
Thompson was dead, leaving Jewitt the sole survivor of the
massacre.

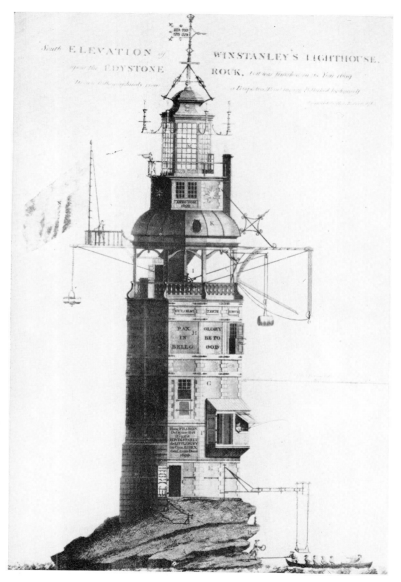

Eddystone Light as it appeared several years before it vanished in the
great storm of 1703, carrying its builder, Henry Winstanley, to his
death. *(Ch. 1)*

The hanging of Ambrose Gwinett *(Ch. 2)*

Philip Quarll with his monkey at the time they were discovered by the Bristol merchant, Edward Dorrington. Quarll had
lived for almost fifty years on an uninhabited South Pacific
island. *(Ch. 3)*

Nootka Indians surround the *Boston* prior to the massacre of her crew. *(Ch. 4)*

Nootka Indians aboard the *Boston (Ch. 4)*

The *Apollo* is lost off the coast of Portugal during a terrible storm in 1804 which destroyed thirty vessels in the area. (*Ch. 5*)

The *Briton* and the *Runnymede* were swept ashore together on the Andaman Islands in the Bay of Bengal during a storm in 1844. (*Ch. 7*)

An albatross aids in the rescue of a drowning soldier. *(Ch. 8)*

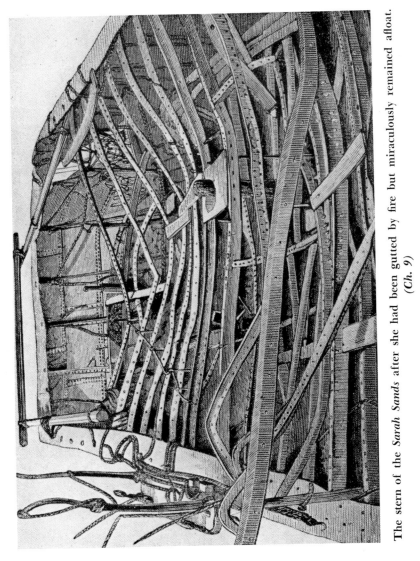

The stern of the *Sarah Sands* after she had been gutted by fire but miraculously remained afloat. *(Ch. 9)*

A sketch of the six boys abandoned on the ice of St. George's Bay, New Foundland, by the captain of the *Arran* in 1868. *(Ch. 12)*

The burial of Abraham Sherrie at sea. *(Ch. 13)*

Captain W. D. Andrews, credited with saving almost fifty persons from drowning, on the way to one of his many rescues. (*Ch. 15*)

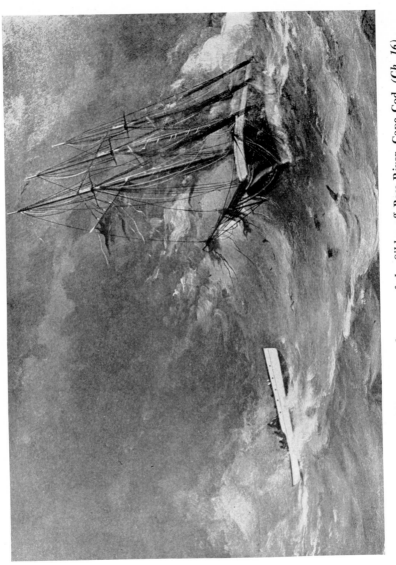

The gasoline boat *Ildico* rescues the crew of the *Sibley* off Bass River, Cape Cod. (*Ch. 16*)

Captain Louis Doucette, hero of many adventures in the Atlantic Ocean, including the rescue of the crew of the *Mertie B. Crowley*.
(Ch. 17)

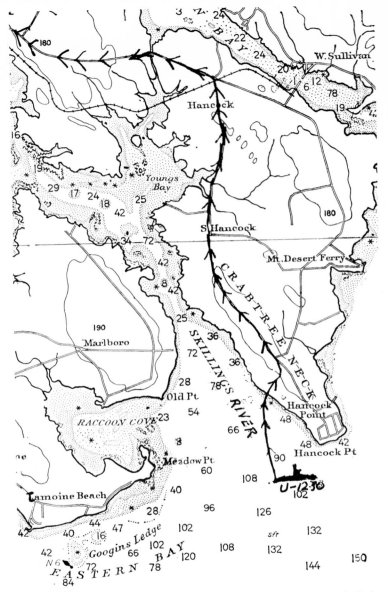

Route used by two German spies who landed at Hancock Point, Maine, from the U-1230 during World War II. *(Ch. 18)*

Mrs. Dante Forni indicates place on the shore of Hancock Point, Maine where the German spies from the U-1230 landed in a rubber raft. *(Ch. 18)*

The schooner *Enchantress,* which vanished without a trace in January, 1964, while sailing from Charleston, South Carolina, to St. Thomas, Virgin Islands. *(Ch. 19)*

Rescue operations in Brisbane Harbor, Australia, where the giant Danish dredge *Kaptajn Nielsen* capsized, trapping twenty-three men below the surface. (*Ch. 20*)

THE *APOLLO*

In the spring of 1804 sixty-nine merchant ships and convoying vessels set sail from Cork, Ireland, bound for the West Indies. Caught in a terrible storm on the eighth day while off the coast of Portugal, no less than thirty vessels were lost in a massive disaster. Ship after ship went aground and broke up on rocks offshore during the gale. Among the wrecked ships was the frigate *Apollo*. Only several officers survived unhurt. One of them, although he identifies other shipmates, left no record of his own name. His narrative is credited to "an officer of the *Apollo*." Thus this extraordinarily vivid account must remain anonymous:

Monday, the 26th of March, sailed from the Cove of Cork, in company with his Majesty's ship *Carysfort*, and 69 sail of merchant ships, under convoy for the West Indies; 27th were out of sight of land, with a fair wind, blowing a strong gale, and steering about W.S.W.; the 28th, 29th and 30th weather and course nearly the same: 31st, the wind came more to the westward, but more moderate. Sunday, the 1st of April at noon, observed in lat. 40 deg. 51 min. North; longitude, per account, 12 deg. 29 min. West; at eight o'clock on Sunday evening the wind shifted to the S.W. blowing fresh; course S.S.E. At ten up mainsail, and set the main stay-sail. At a quarter-past ten the main stay-sail split by the sheeting giving way; called all hands upon deck. At half-past ten strong breezes and squally; took in the fore-top-sail and set the fore-sail. At half-past eleven the main-top-sail split; furled it and the mainsail. The ship was now under her fore-sail, main and mizzen storm-stay-sails; the wind blowing hard, with a very heavy sea.

About half-past three on Monday morning, the 2nd, the ship struck the ground, to the astonishment of every one on board, and the above reckoning, we then conjectured upon an unknown shore. She continued striking the ground very heavily several times, by which her bottom was materially damaged, making much water; the chain pumps were rigged with the utmost dispatch, and the men began to pump, but in about ten minutes she beat and drove over the shoal. On endeavouring to steer her, found the rudder carried away— she then got before the wind; the pumps were kept going, but from the quantity of water she shipped, there was every probability of her soon foundering, as she was filling, and sinking very fast.

After running about five minutes, the ship struck the ground again, with such tremendous shocks, that we were fearful she would instantly go to pieces, and kept striking and driving farther on the sands, the sea making breachs completely over her. Cut away the lanyards of the main and mizzen rigging, and the masts fell with a tremendous crash, over the larboard side; the foremast went immediately after. The ship then fell on her starboard side, with the gunwale under water. The violence with which she struck the ground, and the weight of the guns, those on the quarter deck tearing

away the bulwark, soon made the ship a perfect wreck abaft;
only four or five guns could possibly be fired to alarm the
convoy, and give notice of danger.

On her striking the second time, most pitiful cries were
heard everywhere between decks, many of the men giving
themselves up to inevitable death. I was told I might as well
stay below, as there was an equal likelihood of perishing if I
got upon deck. I was determined to go, but first attempted
to enter my cabin, and was in danger of having my legs
broken by the chests floating about, and the bulk-heads were
giving way; I therefore desisted, and endeavoured to get
upon deck, which I effected, after being several times washed
down. The ship still beating the ground very violently, made
it necessary to cling fast to some part of the wreck, to prevent being washed by the surges, or hurled by the dreadful
concussions overboard; the people holding fast by the larboard bulwark of the quarter deck, and in the main chains,
while our captain stood naked upon the cabin skylight grat-
ing, holding fast by the stump of the mizzen-mast, and making use of every soothing expression which could have been
suggested to encourage men in such a perilous situation.
Most of the officers and men were entirely naked, not having
time to slip on a pair of trousers.

Our horrible situation every moment became more dreadful; until daylight appearing, about half-past four o'clock,
discovered to us the land, at about two cables length, distance, a long sandy beach, reaching to Cape Mondego, three
leagues to the southward of us. On daylight clearing up, we
could perceive between twenty and thirty sail of the convoy
ashore, both to the northward and southward, and several of
them perfect wrecks. We were now certain of being on the
coast of Portugal, from seeing the above Cape, though, I am
sorry to say, no person in the ship had the least idea of being
so near that coast. It blowing hard, and a very great swell of

the sea (or what is generally termed wave running mountains high), there was little prospect of being saved. About eight o'clock there being every likelihood of the ship going to pieces, and the after part lying lowest, Captain Dixon ordered every person forward, which it was very difficult to comply with, from the motion of the mainmast working on the larboard gunwale, there being no other way to get forward. Mr. Cook, the boatswain, had his thigh broken in endeavouring to get a boat over the side; of six fine boats, not one was saved, being all staved, and washed over with the booms, etc.

Soon after the people got forward the ship parted at the gangways. The crew were now obliged to stow themselves in the fore channels, and from thence to the bowsprit end, to the number of 220; for out of 240 persons on board when the ship first struck, I suppose 20 to have previously perished between decks and otherwise. Mr. Lawton, the gunner, the first person who attempted to swim on shore, was drowned; afterwards Lieutenant Wilson, Mr. Runcie, surgeon, Mr. M'Cabe, surgeon's mate, Mr. Stanley, master's mate, and several men shared the same fate, by reason of the sea breaking in enormous surges over them, though excellent swimmers. About 40 persons had the good fortune to reach the shore, upon planks and spars, among whom were Lieutenant Harvey, and Mr. Callam, master's mate. Monday night our situation was truly horrid, the old men and boys dying through hunger and fatigue; also Mr. Proby, and Mr. Hayes, midshipmen. Captain Dixon remained all this night upon the bowsprit.

Tuesday morning presented us no better prospect of being relieved from the jaws of death; the wind blowing stronger and the sea much more turbulent. About noon this day our drooping spirits were somewhat raised by seeing Lieutenant Harvey, and Mr. Callam, hoisting out a boat from one of

the merchant ships to come to the assistance of their distressed shipmates. They several times attempted to launch
her through the surf, but being a very heavy boat, and the sea
on the beach acting so powerfully against them, they could
not possibly effect it, though assisted by nearly 100 men of
the merchant sailors, and Portuguese peasants.

Several men went upon rafts this day, made from pieces
of the wreck, but not one soul reached the shore; the wind
having shifted, and the current setting out, they were all
driven to sea, among whom was our captain, who, about
three in the afternoon, went on the jib-boom with three seamen; anxious to save the remainder of the ship's company,
and too sanguine of getting safe on shore, he ventured upon
the spar, saying, on jumping into the sea—"My lads, I'll save
you all." In a few seconds he lost his hold of the spar, which
he could not regain; he drifted to sea, and perished. Such
was also the fate of the three brave volunteers who chose his
fortune.

The loss of our captain, who, until now, had animated the
almost lifeless crew, as well as the noble exertions of Lieut.
Harvey and Mr. Callam, to launch the boat not succeeding,
every gleam of hope vanished, and we looked forward for certain death, the ensuing night, not only from cold, hunger,
and fatigue, but the expectation of the remaining part of the
wreck going to pieces every moment. Had not the *Apollo*
been a new and well-built ship, that small portion of her
could not have so long resisted the waves, and stuck so well
together, particularly as all the after part from the chesstrees
was gone, the starboard bow under water, the forecastle deck
nearly perpendicular, the weight of the guns hanging to the
larboard bulwark on the outside, which it was not prudent
to cut away, as they afforded resting-places to a considerable
number of men, there being only the fore channels, and cat-
head, where it was possible to live in, and about which were

stowed upwards of 150 men; it being impracticable to continue any longer in the head, or upon the bowsprit, by reason of the breakers washing completely over those places.

The night drawing on, the wind increasing, with frequent showers of rain, the sea washing over us, and looking every instant for the forecastle giving way, when we must have all perished together, afforded a spectacle truly deplorable, the bare recollection of which even now makes me shudder. The piercing cries of the people this dismal night, at every sea coming over them, which happened every two minutes, were painful in the extreme; the water running from the head all down over the body, keeping us continually wet. This shocking night the remaining strength of every person was exerted for his individual safety. From the crowding so closely together, in such a narrow compass, and the want of something to moisten their mouths, several poor wretches were suffocated; which frequently reminded me of the Black Hole, with this only difference, that those poor sufferers were confined by strong walls, we by water; the least movement, without clinging fast, would have launched us into eternity. Some unfortunate wretches drank salt water, several their own urine, some chewed leather, myself and many more chewed lead, from which we conceived we found considerable relief, by reason of its drawing the saliva, which we swallowed. In less than an hour after the ship first struck the ground, all the provisions were under water, and the ship a wreck, so that it was impossible to procure any part.

After the most painful night that is possible to conceive, on day-light appearing, we observed Lieut. Harvey and Mr. Callam again endeavouring to launch the boat. Several attempts were made without success, a number of men belonging to the merchant ships being much bruised and hurt in assisting; alternate hopes and fears now pervaded our wretched minds; fifteen men got safe on shore this morning on pieces of the wreck. About three in the afternoon, of Wednesday the 4th, we had the inexpressible happiness of seeing the boat launched through the surf, by the indefatigable exertion of the brave officers, assisted by the masters of the merchant ships, with a number of Portuguese peasants, who were encouraged by Mr. Whitney, the British Consul, from Figueras.

All the crew then remaining on the wreck were brought safe on shore, praising God for a happy deliverance from a shipwreck which has scarcely ever had its parallel. As soon as I stept out of the boat, I found several persons whose humanity prompted them to offer me sustenance, though improperly, in spirits, which I avoided as much as possible.

Our weak state may be conceived, when it is considered that we received no nourishment from Sunday to Wednesday afternoon, and were continually exposed to the fury of the watery element. After eating and drinking a little, I found myself weaker than before, occasioned, I apprehend, from having been so long without either. Some men died soon after getting on shore, from imprudently drinking too large a quantity of spirits. All the crew were in a very weak and exhausted state, the greater part being badly bruised and wounded. About thirty sail of merchant ships were wrecked at the same time on this dreadful beach. Some ships sunk with all their crew, and almost every ship lost from two to twelve men each; yet the situation of the remainder was not equally distressing with that of the crew of the frigate; as the merchant ships drawing a less draught of water, were mostly driven close on shore, and no person remained on board them after the first morning.

The masters of the merchant ships had tents upon the beach, and some provisions which they had saved from the wrecks, which they very generously distributed, and gave every assistance to the *Apollo*'s crew. Thus was lost one of the finest frigates in the British navy, with sixty-one of her crew. The number of souls lost in the merchant ships was also very considerable. Dead bodies were every day floating on shore, and pieces of wreck covered the beach ten miles in extent.

This fatal and unprecedented calamity is universally ascribed to the carelessness and inattention of the Commodore, and it is asserted, that had it been dark a quarter of an hour longer, the whole convoy would have shared the same fate.

6

RICHARD HOODLASS,
THE HORSE-SWIMMER

All too often I read stories of the villainous customs of mooncussers and wreckers luring vessels to their doom by displaying false lights along the shore. On the other side of the ledger I have discovered an English farmer who more than a century ago saved the lives of many people by riding his horse directly into the waves to reach vessels wrecked in the area.

This brave man, named Richard Hoodlass, was a farmer near Grainthrope on the coast of Lincolnshire. For many years he devoted himself to the saving of mariners from drowning, without any of the usual apparatus for aiding survivors aboard wrecked vessels. Unaided and usually unaccompanied by any living creature but his horse, he was the means of rescuing many unfortunate sailors from perishing amidst the waves.

Hoodlass cultivated a small piece of ground on a peninsula jutting out into the sea. Since there were no good roads in this area, he knew that in a storm he was the only one who could save any unfortunates wrecked in a gale. He took it upon himself in stormy weather to scan the sea for a sign of vessels in distress. He cut an opening through the roof at the top of his dwelling, and there built a small but sturdy cupola. Whenever a storm came up, he would climb up to his perch, point his telescope toward the ocean, and watch the approach of vessels toward the rocky shore.

In threatening weather, night and day, he visited the cupola, training his spyglass on the sea. Whenever he discovered a ship struggling offshore, he would make his plans for rescue. When all on board might have given themselves up for lost, he was ready to risk his life. Climbing down into the house, he would discard his telescope and don his heavy gear.

Then mounting his faithful horse, Hoodlass would start out to the wreck. Accustomed to the salt water missions, the animal swam and plunged, only turning for an instant when a wave threatened to swallow it.

Reaching the doomed craft, Hoodlass often managed to save two or three mariners at once, riding them ashore. Then he would return for another load. Again and again he would repeat his rescue work until all aboard were either saved or drowned, as he often could not save all the victims in time.

Once, when he was questioned about the horse after a particularly thrilling rescue, he explained that in reality no training was necessary, for all depended upon the skill and firmness of the rider. Hoodlass stated that he could manage the most unruly horse once it was over its head in water; for as soon as the animal found that it had lost its footing, it became as obedient to the bridle as a boat is to its helm. When meeting a particularly gigantic swell, he turned his horse's head away, bent forward, and allowed the wave to roll over them to prevent the water from entering the animal's nostrils.

In my research I discovered that the first time he attracted the attention of others was in the year 1833, when he swam his horse through a stormy sea to the wreck of the *Hermione*. In the company of a friend, also mounted on horseback, he saved half her crew, for which gallant service they afterward received testimonials from the Royal Humane Society. The words of the resolution passed by the society on this occasion follow:

> It was resolved unanimously that the noble courage and humanity displayed by Richard Hoodlass for the preservation of the crew of the *Hermione* from drowning, when the vessel was wrecked near Donna Nook, on the coast of Lincolnshire, on the 31st of August, 1833, and the praiseworthy manner in which he risked his life on that occasion, by swimming his horse through a heavy sea to the wreck, *when it was found impossible* to launch the life-boat, has called for the lively admiration of the special general court, and justly entitles him to the honorary medallion of the institution, which is hereby adjudged to be presented to him at the ensuing anniversary festival.

A similar medal was presented to his friend, Joseph Dobson, who moved inland a relatively short time later and thus became unable to participate in further lifesaving activities.

On one occasion Hoodlass saved not only the captain of a vessel and his wife, but no less than ten seamen—some of them on the back of the horse, and others by hanging on the stirrups. It was a remarkable feat of daring.

If a vessel were lying on her beam ends, Hoodlass was forced to exercise extreme caution in making his approach, because of the lines and rigging concealed in the water. One day he experienced great difficulty. He had secured two seamen and was attempting to leave the vessel for the shore, but the horse could not get away. After various plunges underwater, Hoodlass discovered that the animal was entangled in a rope.

The seas were furious and to dismount was impossible. Fortunately, he was able at length to pick up the rope with his foot. Then instantly pulling a knife from his pocket, he leaned forward into the water, cut the line, and was able to guide his horse ashore safely.

Following is the correspondence recommending Hoodlass and his companion for testimonials:

⚓

To the Secretary of the Royal Humane Society

Bolton House, 29th Jan. 1834

Sir,

It had been my fixed intention to made an application to the Royal Humane Society, on behalf of two men, namely, Richard Hoodlass and Joseph Dobson, who, in the most gallant manner, saved the lives of four out of eight, forming the crew of a brig that was stranded on the coast of Lincolnshire during the dreadful storm of the 31st of August last; and who very nobly declined receiving any portion of a sum, which I immediately sent for the reward of those who had exerted themselves on that occasion; saying, it was a sufficient satisfaction to them to have been able, under the blessing of Providence, to save the lives of four fellow-creatures. I take blame to myself for not having sooner made this case known to you, but I was under the full impression, that no decision was made by the Society till near the time of the Anniversary Meeting, which is usually towards the end of April; and that, therefore, it would be unnecessary to lay the statement before the Committee, till about the time of the meeting of Parliament, when I might probably be in town myself, and could personally bring the case under their notice. I was greatly surprised, therefore, to find, by a statement in the newspaper about a fortnight ago, that the Annual Meeting for the Adjudication of Rewards had already taken place, and I requested my brother, Sir Edward Cust, to make enquiry of you on this subject. Since the receipt of his answer, I have lost no time in procuring the precise facts of this case from C. B. Massingberd, Esq., my Deputy Vice-Admiral, whose report I herewith enclose. I most earnestly hope, that under all the circumstances, it may not be considered too late to include those two men in the list of those who may receive medals from the Society next April; for, as their conduct is so *highly deserving of commendation* it would be a great mortification to myself to find, that by an accidental oversight of my own, they should be deprived of an honourable mark of distinction which would prove highly gratifying to them.

I have the honour, &c.

——————————————————— (Signed)   Brownlow.

I hereby certify, that Richard Hoodlass and Joseph Dobson, both inhabitants of Summer Coats, hearing that the brig *Hermione,* of Sunderland, Captain Wilton, was stranded near Donner Rock, on the Lincolnshire coast, on the 31st day of August, 1833, when not being able to get the life-boat to sea, most bravely rode into the sea up to the wreck, swimming their horses a part of the way, and brought away four out of eight of the crew, each taking a man before him and another behind him, when the brig upset and the rest of the crew were drowned.

C. B. Massingberd,
Deputy Vice-Admiral

Ormsby Hall
28 Jan. 1834

7

TWO SHIPWRECKS

Although there have been thousands and thousands of shipwrecks in the world's history, only on rare occasions have two craft in the same storm smashed ashore almost side by side on a far-flung island.

The location of the two shipwrecks, the *Briton* and the *Runnymede,* is the Andaman Islands south of Rangoon in the Bay of Bengal. One of the ship's company on the *Briton* later wrote of his experience, but his name has not come down to us.

"In the year 1844 I was on board the *Briton,* a ship of 600 tons built at Sydney in Australia, from which port we sailed in October to Calcutta, conveying a wing of the 80th regiment which had been stationed for some time in the colony. They mustered about 400 officers and men, many of whom had also their wives and children with them."

The first part of the voyage was fine, but on the morning of November 7, when they reached the Bay of Bengal, a heavy gale sprang up. On the tenth it became a regular hurricane. They could scarcely show a stitch of canvas before it was blown away. Everyone knew that the Andaman Islands, surrounded by reefs and inhabited by fierce savages, were

dead ahead. The soldiers and the women and children were
sent below and the hatches battened down over them. Life-
lines were stretched fore and aft. Tremendous seas began to
break completely over the ship, sweeping everything from
the decks. All boats, caboose, and bulwarks were washed
away, and on many occasions when the ship buried itself
beneath the waves, it appeared that she would never rise
again.

The report continues: "Early in the forenoon watch when
everyone was struggling against the mountainous billows, a
furious blast struck us, and away went the foremast crashing
over the side."

Then the mainmast and finally the mizzenmast went over.
When night came on, the seas were as bad as ever. Soon it
was so black that no one could see beyond the foaming billows which rose up on either side. Hour after hour passed.
Then, during the morning watch, the *Briton* ground ashore
on a rocky ledge, slid across, and shuddered to a stop.

Shrieks of terror came from below. Husbands and wives
now took a last farewell of each other and of their children.
The *Briton*, however, refused to go to pieces. Another great
billow formed, reared high in the sky, and roared shoreward.
The mighty wave smashed against the craft and pushed her
off the ledge. Caught in the mighty comber as though she
were a tiny surfboard, the vessel began a weird trip toward
shore. Suddenly she fetched up. Miraculously, as lightning
flashes revealed, the sailors saw that the wave had transported
the *Briton* with her hundreds of passengers right to the edge
of a forest of coconut trees, just above the jagged rocks of the
shore.

The sailors took off the hatches and told everyone below
that they would probably be able to get ashore. The decision
was made, however, to keep all on board at least until an
exploration of the shore was attempted.

To their utter surprise, when morning came they saw the masts and spars of another ship rising above the ledges scarcely more than four hundred yards away. She was fast on the reef and crowded with men. As the sea was beating violently over her, it was recorded, "We felt great fear for her safety." Those on the other craft had made no attempt to get ashore, but as the weather moderated and the sea fell, "we went over and opened a conversation with them, finding that she was the *Runnymede* a transport of 500 tons, and she had left England * in August bound for Calcutta with a large number of recruits for the 50th regiment."

Neither craft had seen the other until the dawn of that day when they were wrecked so close to each other. It blew very hard for the next few days, but there was no danger of the *Runnymede* going to pieces, and the people stayed on board. Every time the tide went out the *Briton* was left on practically dry ground. The soldiers were landed, and the men set off an area of the jungle. First they cut down the shrubbery, and then they burned the debris.

A few days later they had convincing proof that the island was inhabited, when they saw a number of dark objects in the distance. A moment or two went by, and then a shower of arrows came in among the working party on the outskirts of the encampment. Two of the party were hit, and it was not until a volley from the muskets of the soldiers was fired at the enemy that they took flight. They returned, however, again and again, and not until several had been killed did they decide to keep at a respectful distance. Even then they were seen hovering about ready to pick off any stragglers who might venture away from camp.

The Andaman Islands are rarely visited because of the cannibals who inhabit them, and the shipwrecked officers

---

* Owned by Messrs. Halland Co. of London, she had sailed from the Downs.

realized that their chief hope of escaping was by communicating with some friendly port. Unfortunately, only one boat from the two ships could be made fit for a voyage across the Bay of Bengal. After undergoing repairs, she was ready for the journey. It was decided that the master of the *Briton*, the mate of the *Runnymede*, and several seamen would sail her to the nearest port, which was Mergui. Everyone went down to the beach when they sailed away and sent them off with anxious prayers for their safety.

Meanwhile regular military discipline was maintained. The island on which they were cast forms one of an archipelago about 12° north of the equator in longitude 93° 13' east. The largest of the group is the Great Andaman, 140 miles long and 20 wide, with deep bays and long creeks. There are smaller islands, of course, covered with tropical vegetation reaching in unrestrained profusion from the level swamps to the highest hills in all directions. Coral reefs go out for many miles, making it difficult to land in blowing weather.

The aborigines are perhaps the best bowmen among all tribes of savages. Their bows are six feet long, of great power, and "the strongest men among us were unable to bend the weapon which these little fellows used with the greatest of ease." They are remarkably small, the men seldom taller than five feet and the women still shorter. They wear no clothes whatever, merely putting on layers of mud to keep off the flies and the mosquitoes. They also have harpoons which they shoot from their bows for catching fish, with one end of a line attached to the harpoon, and the other held by the archer. They construct outrigger canoes which they use to go as far as forty or fifty miles to sea. Fire, with which to cook fish, is taken aboard these craft.

The natives do not habitually devour human flesh, and only when pressed by hunger do they succumb to cannibalism. Fear of all foreigners, however, induces them to attack with the greatest fierceness anyone visiting their shores. They fearfully mutilate the bodies of all whom they may kill.

Living principally on fish and fruits, they also have a race of tiny black pigs, the most curious and mischievous creatures to be seen. "There is a peculiar leer in their eyes which showed the evil spirit within them." The pigs' backs are sprinkled with hard bristles which are like pieces of wire. When hunted, though they may at first take to flight, back they come and run between the hunter's legs, sometimes tripping him and then often making their getaway. The pigs are delightful to eat when cooked in ovens, prepared in a simple and ingenious fashion. To form one of these ovens, a large tree is chosen and fire is applied to some hole a little above the ground. By degrees the hole is burned larger, and the charred wood is scraped out, leaving a hollow of considerable size. At the bottom of the hole a heap of hot ashes about three feet deep is left. Thus whenever a native wishes to cook his dinner, he has only to blow up the smoldering embers and place the pig or fish on top of them. The inhabitants carefully preserve the oven trees and manage to keep them from burning through as long as they can.

The people from the *Briton* and *Runnymede* had very little intercourse with the Andaman Islanders. Although superior to some of the tribes found in Australia in some respects, they are infinitely more savage and less tamable than most.

As the weeks passed, the crews of the two ships became concerned for the safe return of the officers and sailors, and prayed they had reached Mergui. Their provisions were beginning to grow short, and their anxiety was increasing when a schooner was discerned in the offing.

The reporter wrote: "We eagerly watched her; she approached. At length she came to anchor, and a boat coming on shore, we found she was the company's schooner *George Swinton* and that she had brought us a welcome supply of provisions. In a short time Her Majesty's steamer *Ganges* and a brig-of-war arrived, followed by two other vessels which had been chartered to convey the troops and crews of the wrecked ships to Calcutta, as well as everything belonging to them which could be carried away."

So little damage had the *Briton* received that could she have been launched, she might have been refitted, and continued on her voyage, but this was found impossible, so they set fire to her in order to prevent the natives from obtaining possession of the hull. The *Runnymede,* which lay near the outer part of the reef, had become a total loss. The troops reached Calcutta in safety, many of the poor fellows being destined shortly to leave their bones on the great battlefields of the Sutlej.

The boat had taken a month to reach Mergui. The company schooner *George Swinton* was dispatched with provisions to the islands, and in the course of the week five other vessels were sent to the aid of the distressed troops, two of them belonging to the Royal Navy. They were the steamer *Ganges* and the war brig *Pilot.* The other vessels were the *Ayreshire,* the *Agnes Lee,* and the *Elizabeth Amelia.*

The instructions were that upon their arrival they were to take the troops from both ships on board and to go with them direct to Calcutta, and the remainder were to take the crew and save as much of the vessels as they possibly could.

It was agreed that had those on board the *Briton* and the *Runnymede* been defenseless immigrants instead of troops, they would have been speedily butchered.

8

SAVED BY AN ALBATROSS

From time to time I have read unusual stories about the sea in which a drowning man is pushed ashore by a friendly dolphin, or a bird in some strange way brings aid to a castaway on an island. Two stories in this chapter involve an albatross, and another one concerns a strange bird that caused a sea captain to change his route while at sea.

About seventy years ago an albatross was found choking to death by two boys on a beach in Freemantle, Australia. Before they could help it the bird died. Examination of the corpse revealed a metal collar which had been forced around its neck. The collar was made from a tin can. Letters scratched in the tin with a sharp instrument formed the words:

> *Treize naufrages sont refugies sur les Iles Crozetes.*
> *Au Secours pour l'amour de Dieu.*

Translated, the message indicated that thirteen sailors were on the Crozet Islands and needed help.

The plea had been written only twelve days before it was discovered, but official regulations delayed for many weeks the sending of a rescue party to the islands, which were located some thousand miles from Australia. Finally, after a long delay, a boat was put ashore at the uninhabited Crozet Islands, and the crew came upon the location where the thirten Frenchmen had been marooned. All that remained was another message to the effect that the thirteen men were out of food and had sailed away for help, actually a short time before the rescue group arrived. The Frenchmen evidently perished at sea, for they were never heard from again.

It is unfortunate that such a clever attempt to attract attention to their unhappy predicament should fail because of governmental red tape and bungling. If the rescue ship had been sent at once, all thirteen men would have been saved.

Another strange story concerns Captain Johnson of the Norwegian bark *Ellen,* who was standing on the quarterdeck on the afternoon of September 12, 1857. His words follow:

Suddenly a bird flew around me, first grazing my right shoulder. It soon flew at my face, when I caught hold of it, and made it a prisoner. The bird was unlike any bird I ever saw, nor do I know its name. As it strove to bite everybody, I had its head cut off, and the body thrown overboard. When the bird flew to the ship, the bark was going a little eastward of northeast.

I regarded the appearance of the bird as an omen, and an indication to me that I must change my course. I accordingly headed to the eastward direct. I should not have deviated from my course, had not the bird visited the ship, and, had not it been for this change of course, I should not have fallen in with the 49 passengers, whom I fortunately saved from certain death.

⚓

The passengers were from the steamer *Central America,* which had foundered.

One of the most singular rescues concerning birds at sea occurred around the year 1850. For some trifling dereliction of duty a soldier aboard a ship on its way to the Orient was ordered to be severely flogged. The punishment was carried out with great cruelty, and the man was soon driven to madness by the pain and disgrace.

When he was released from the cords which bound him, he ran screaming across to the bulwarks of the vessel. Before any member of the ship's crew or his fellow soldiers could stop him, he jumped onto the taffrail. For a moment he stood there. Then he turned around to his torturers and shouted: "You will regret this act." Finally, he faced the ocean and gave a long leap into the sea.

As the crew watched his body splash into the waves far below there was a rush to lower the nearest boat. Unfortunately the seas were running high, and as the soldier disappeared into the distance all hope of saving him appeared to be at an end.

While members of the crew were still vainly struggling to lower the boat, a huge bird, soon identified as an albatross, was seen in the distance swooping down over the area where the man was struggling for his life in the water. As the form of the soldier grew more indistinct in the distance, the bird apparently fluttered lower and lower over him.

The vessel was put about and the boat, which was finally lowered, began to approach the scene where the albatross was still hovering over what apparently was the man. Rowing closer and closer the men in the lifeboat soon came upon a scene which, although they saw it, they could not believe. In some way the man had grasped the bird's two legs, one in his left hand and one in his right, and in spite of the bird's agonized struggles, the soldier retained his grasp.

As the lifeboat drew closer and closer the bird fluttered vainly in an attempt to escape. Finally the crew drew alongside the soldier and grasped his arms, whereupon he released his hold on the huge albatross, which was allowed to fly away, having saved a human life.

THE MIRACLE OF THE
SARAH SANDS

What is the most astounding sea holocaust in the world's history? In my opinion, neither the size of the ship nor the number of people lost should decide this, but rather what transpired aboard the unfortunate vessel.

In many of my other books I have told the classic stories of ships burning at sea. They include the loss of the *Kent,* the *Royal Tar,* the *Lexington,* the *General Slocum,* and the *Morro Castle.**

When the *Kent* burned at sea in March, 1825, this 1,350-ton East Indiaman had 641 persons aboard, of whom 69 died. Eleven years later off the shores of Maine the circus ship *Royal Tar* burned and sank near Isle au Haut with 32 of the 93 members of the ship's company perishing along with most of the animals. In 1840 the *Lexington,* out of New York, burned and sank in Long Island Sound with the loss of 150 people; barely a handful escaped. On June 15, 1904, 1,600 passengers went aboard the *General Slocum* in New York

* The *Kent* and *Morro Castle* appear in my *Great Gales and Dire Disasters;* the *Royal Tar* in *True Tales of Terrible Shipwrecks;* the *Lexington* in *Storms and Shipwrecks;* and the *General Slocum* in *Secrets of the North Atlantic Islands.*

Harbor. A few hours later, 1,031 had died in the fire that developed. On Friday night, September 7, 1934, the great luxury liner *Morro Castle* caught fire while off the shores of New Jersey, and before she eventually grounded near Asbury Park the next morning, 134 of the 562 people aboard had died!

I have cited typical examples of what fire can do to a vessel out on the rolling main and also in sheltered harbors. Joseph Conrad once said that "the ocean has that conscienceless temper of a savage autocrat spoiled by much adulation," while Lord Byron insisted that "ten thousand fleets" might sweep over the ocean "in vain." It was true, Byron explained, that although "man marks the earth with ruin; his control stops with the shore."

Keeping in mind what these two great writers say, I believe that the story of the *Sarah Sands* is the exception which proves the rule.

When the *Sarah Sands* burned at sea in 1857, not only did her crew and passengers manage to save her and bring the ship to port, but not one person died as a result of the terrible fire which practically destroyed her stern and amidships section! At the time of the disaster it was agreed among men of the sea that the escape from this holocaust was most remarkable. Later historian Walter Wood spoke of this conflagration as "the most disastrous that any ship ever survived."

Without question, the "heroic labour and indomitable courage of officers and men of the 54th Regiment . . . were deciding factors in saving the transport *Sarah Sands*."

England was then in the throes of putting down a great rebellion of the native troops in India.* In 1857 the Sepoy

---

* The mutiny was triggered by the introduction of a greased cartridge which the native troops believed was greased with cow's fat. The troops had to bite the cartridge before they fired it, and the Mohammedan troops were defiled when they bit the cartridge, while the Hindus thought themselves guilty of sacrilege.

regiments of Calcutta and Delhi mutinied and soon most of northern India was in revolt. The slaughter of Cawnpore was the worst tragedy.

England, desperate for ships to carry troops to India, hired or bought outright scores of craft which had seen better days. There was also a shortage of men to sail those ships, and many captains were forced to sign on convicts and scum from the waterfront who ordinarily would not have been considered. It became so bad that any man who called himself a sailor, whether he qualified or not, was certain of employment.

With such a crew, the *Sarah Sands* had started out from England, her purpose to land troops to help quell the Indian mutiny. For two weary months, the *Sands* had forced her way south from the British Isles, so that by the time she was approaching Cape Town, she needed more coal and supplies. Her master, Captain Castle, already burdened with an undesirable and mutinous crew, decided to put in to Cape Town for the needed supplies.

The crew, nearly half of whom were foreigners, became so boisterous at Cape Town that many were put in jail and then taken to the ship in irons.

Finally the *Sarah Sands* left Cape Town for Calcutta with 500 souls aboard. Among these were 358 soldiers to put down the mutiny in India, and a number of women and children. A dozen of the ship's crew were still held in irons for their own mutinous conduct. The route of the ship was past Ceylon and through the Indian Ocean and the Bay of Bengal to Calcutta.

One day a young Dutchman in the crew, always cheerful and full of fun, walked along the rail and lost his balance when the ship gave a sudden roll. Into the sea he fell with a splash and never came to the surface. His cap was all that ever appeared! As sharks swarmed about the transport, one of them probably devoured the young man. There were many who said later that a curse was on the vessel from the very outset.

The mutineers, confined below, had been kept on bread and water for seven days. In some way, it was later claimed, the mutineers started the mysterious fire which nearly brought about the destruction of the *Sarah Sands* and all on board.

Heavily laden when leaving the Cape, deep with coal, fresh water, and stores, the steamship had driven into bad weather almost at once.

On the afternoon of November 11, 1857, the *Sands* had reached a position a thousand miles out from the Cape of Good Hope. The men were smoking their pipes and sitting about, chatting and laughing and passing the time in pleasant fashion.

Private George Diggens, who wrote of the fire years later when he was a patient at Chelsea Hospital, states that while aboard the ship he was a rather favored person, because, as servant to Dr. O'Donovan, he was allowed an extra pint of porter * daily. That afternoon he went below to get his pint and was instantly met by an awful smell of something burning. Knowing too well the terrible danger if fire broke out, he dashed to the hatchway where he met the carpenter about to descend.

"I believe the ship's on fire," Diggens shouted.

"Shut up!" the carpenter answered. "You'll be put in irons if you say that!"

Nevertheless, the carpenter hurried below, after which he rushed back again, followed almost instantly by Captain Castle and the chief mate.

It was not possible to hide the awful truth. The *Sarah*

---

* Porter is a 4 per cent stout, not to be confused with port, a 20 per cent wine.

Sands was burning, and every soul on board would realize the fact within a short time. Captain Castle ordered the hatches closed down so that no unnecessary draft should feed the fire, but it was already clear that astern the transport was a roaring inferno!

Without the slightest warning the soldiers had been plunged from peace and safety into tumult and peril. They were now about to fight a battle in which the odds were "crushingly against" them. Now came the test of courage, endurance, and the steadying power of discipline. What of the mutineers, the foreigners, who knew neither drill nor obedience, and who had no *esprit de corps* to hold them to their duty? In some way, all except one had freed themselves and made a rush for the boats. They jumped into them and, caring for nothing except saving their own skins, pushed off from the *Sarah Sands.*

In the confusion a few of the 54th had jumped into the boats and were carried away from the ship's side. The eleven women and children aboard were hurried into one of the craft. In it, covered with blankets and comforters, they were huddled during those long, awful hours of daylight and darkness in which the men struggled to beat out the flames and save the ship. The weather was growing worse, with the boats thrown about by the seas. One lifeboat was swamped, but no lives were lost, as the occupants were taken back aboard the ship.

When the fire broke out, the *Sarah Sands* had been carrying sail. The commander ordered all sails furled and also directed that the ship be swung around and kept headed into the wind so that the fire would be confined to the afterpart of the transport. This would have been a hard task with so few sailors left on board, but during the long voyage some of the soldiers had picked up a little seamanship; and so under the direction of the ship's officers, the soldiers managed it.

Hosepipes fitted to the fire engine sprayed the fire; buckets and anything from which water could be thrown were furiously at work. They did everything that mortal men could do to drown the flames, and yet the puny streams had not the least effect on them.

Private George Diggens writes as follows:

Merciful indeed it is that at such times great exertions keep us from dwelling overmuch on what may seem our hopeless case. If there had been a chance for thought, for calculating the overwhelming odds against us, there were not many even of the bravest who would not have resignedly awaited the end, and prayed for its speedy coming; but every man was alert and working, and like very fiends the 54th laboured for the preservation of the *Sarah Sands*.

Even at time of the greatest peril some unexpected incident will force us to the thought of matters other than our personal doings. Here were we, overshadowed by present horrors and the prospect of an almost certain death; yet there arose a strange forgetfulness of self and a concern for the welfare of a fellow-creature. And who was he? Where was he that he should claim attention then, of all times? Where could he have been for his case to be worse than our own plight?

He was a prisoner below, a mutineer in irons, and he was captive in the very heart of that fiery furnace!

This seemed the very crowning horror of our case. He was a sailor—a one-eyed man, called Scottie, the best of the crew; and there he was, helpless below. Instantly there were men willing to risk their lives to try to save him; but no man was allowed to make the attempt; all that we were permitted to do was to throw a rope down in the feeble hope that he could help himself.

A rope was lowered, and Scottie managed to seize it. Then we dragged him up to the deck, irons and all, and he got his poor chance of life like the rest of us. But there were few who thought he could pull round, for he was so overcome with exhaustion that he lay on the deck like one dead, and it was fully twenty minutes before he recovered consciousness.

First and foremost to the soldier of the old days came the thought of his regimental colours. Ours were in the saloon, and the saloon was astern, where the fire was raging. Who would venture on such a forlorn hope as the attempt to save them? Who, indeed? Why, there was an instant dash for them, without thought of personal danger, in defiance of the stifling smoke and scorching flames.

First of all, the two ensigns into whose special care the colours had been given—Lieutenants Houston and Hughes—rushed into the choking saloon and tried to seize them and bring them out. They failed, and barely escaped with their lives.

Then a gallant fellow named Richard Richmond, one of the ship's quartermasters, vanished into the dense smoke and struggled towards the far end of the saloon, where the colours hung. He had a wet cloth over his face, and was armed with an axe. With frantic cuts he got the colours down and staggered back through the suffocating atmosphere. Then, overcome with the heat and smoke, he fainted, and it seemed as if his death was as sure as the destruction of the colours and the ship.

But pluck begets pluck. There was another rush, and Private William Wiles dragged Richmond and the colours from the saloon and on to the deck. They came out of that awful furnace with just strength enough to hold the colours up so that the 54th should see them, and in that thrilling act, and with our cheers ringing in their ears, they fell down senseless and exhausted. Those colours are now in Norwich Cathedral.

↩

The rescue of the colors and the fine example of the regimental officers, whose pluck was as remarkable as their endurance, cheered the men. They had no human enemy to deal with, but there were two foes who had it all their own way—the roaring wind and high seas were in league.

The soldiers were ordered to march and countermarch along the deck and then below. Crowded on the cramped forepart of the ship, the soldiers were continually passing each other. Some were coming up from below, where they had been sent to work, marching forward and meeting the sections who were coming down to relieve those already below.

Private Diggens' report continues:

⚓

It seems easy to talk about pouring water on the fire, but no tongue can tell the difficulties we had to meet and overcome. Before we could get below we had to cut holes in the deck with hatchets; then to grope and stifle in the dense, hot depths, feeling with our hands for the hottest places on the iron plates, and throwing water on to keep them cool. A ceaseless wetting of the coals was also necessary to keep them from bursting into flames.

We crawled and crept and staggered blindly from spot to spot with our buckets and other things, always to keep the fire to its huge metal grate and prevent it from bursting out into the whole of our home.

We never stopped throwing the water down, and never

ceased to pump it up again, so that the *Sarah Sands* should not meet her doom from her only means of preservation.

Now that we were accustomed to the first great danger, we were confronted with another and more awful peril, and that was our destruction by the explosion of the powder in our two magazines.

We had many barrels of gunpowder on board, and in addition, there were the ship's rockets in another magazine. Not even the bravest could think of this new peril without fear; but the terror disappeared in the excitement of getting at the casks.

To get at the starboard powder magazine the men had to be lowered with ropes through the holes in the deck into the suffocating, blistering depths, there to fasten other ropes round powder casks, which would be hauled up.

Each cask as it was landed on the deck was quickly thrown overboard. One by one they came, with the men working until they fainted at their efforts, but at last the starboard magazine was empty.

The port-quarter magazine was still untouched, and it was very near the fire. It could be reached only by one hatchway, and that was already belching dense clouds of hot smoke.

At the call for volunteers, soldiers responded at once. It was absolutely essential to reach the powder and throw it over before it exploded. Again men went below and labored until they fainted, but one by one they threw the casks into the sea. At last there remained one cask of ammunition, some signaling powder, and two large barrels of powder which it was impossible to reach.

As Diggens described it:

⚓

We had so far escaped the fire and kept it to the stern; but the ship was still manageable, and might be saved. But the powder was certain to explode and there was no one who believed that the *Sarah Sands* would survive the explosion.

We had been striving for hours, darkness had settled on the sea, and it seemed as if nothing could be done. The boats —can you imagine the feelings of the unhappy women and children in them, separated from husbands and fathers, tossed on the waters and expecting certain death?—were ordered to get clear of the ship so as to escape the explosion, and they pulled away.

No words can indicate the sufferings of those who waited in the boats and in the ship for the awful end—agonies which were intensified by the enforced partings.

☞

Still trying to save the ship, the men cut away the deck fittings which might catch fire, and cabins and much of the lumber went overboard. They collected the spars and some lumber to make three rafts. When these were constructed, two of them were set afloat, and the third was left across the deck, ready to be lowered at the very last.

To the glory of the 54th be it said that not even then, in the very face of death, knowing that the ship might explode at any moment, did a single soldier rush for the rafts. The troops remained obedient, and the officers continued to encourage and lead them.

It was about this time that brave but exhausted Captain Castle abandoned hope. On the bridge with the doctor he turned to Major Brett, who was in command of the soldiers.

"You have done all you can; nothing more is possible." Then in dramatic fashion he took a pair of marine glasses which were slung over his shoulders. Flinging them into the heart of the fire, he cried out, "They're no good now!"

But Major Brett answered, "We shall never stop working till we're driven overboard!"

In the darkness of the night the flames leaped skyward in spectacular fashion, for the afterpart of the ship was then one mass of fire. The deck had burned away revealing the white-hot iron beams. Indeed it was a weird, eerie scene. To the roaring of the fire, wind, and sea there was the accompaniment of an unearthly light for miles around. The sky was a vast red dome. The sea, swarming with sharks, presented a pink, ghastly reflection.

Suddenly the tarred mizzen rigging took fire. The ropes swiftly burned away, and down crashed the mast. The men fought on, with hose and bucket, still keeping the *Sarah Sands*'s head to wind. The fire was confined to the afterpart of the ship, although once or twice blasts of flame and smoke swept along the length of the transport.

According to Diggens:

We had been striving for many long hours. Man after man had fallen senseless, dropping exhausted on the deck, and the only thing even the doctor could do was to throw salt water on their faces to bring them round.

Our uniforms were scorched from our bodies, our skins were burnt and black with smoke, and we were parched with torturing thirst. Believe me, so terrible was this thirst that our tongues were swollen out of our mouths, and could be forced back only by the pressure of our hands. And there was no relief for us, because our food and drink were being destroyed with our ship.

Suddenly there was the terrible climax for which we had all been waiting. Right astern there was a mighty red flash upwards, a deafening crash, a crackling as if the very elements were dissolving, then a shuddering, sickening sinking of our water-laden troopship.

The powder had exploded at last, and with it had burst the ship's rockets, making such a firework show as never mortal man had seen, I think, for he had never witnessed it in such a setting—and such a one as I have no desire to look upon again.

Not a human being in the transport who felt the shock, not a wretched soul in the boats who saw the awful sight, believed that the vessel would survive, and yet when the shudder had passed through her, when she had recovered from that sickening dip, the *Sarah Sands* rode still, although the wreckage of her stern cabins had been blown out and into fragments and a great hole torn in her port quarter as far down as the water-line.

Marvelous to tell, the explosion injured only two amongst us—a lieutenant and a corporal, who were blown down a hatchway, but were rescued.

The *Sarah Sands*, although the explosion had almost sent her to the bottom, was still afloat. The soldiers went into the fight again with fresh hearts, passing buckets of water and playing hoses on the hot coal and the heated plates. The officers and men hoped that even then they might prevent the fire from spreading. A short time later their efforts triumphed, and they first contained the fire and then put it out.

Throughout that unspeakable night the 54th fought on, unaided by the cowards who had mutinied and left the ship. The officers shouted for the mutineers to come and take the *Sarah Sands* in tow, in order to keep her head to the wind, but they refused, and it was not until all danger from the fire was over that they came on board again. They were jeered at and sneered at when they finally rowed to the ship.

The sharks had tried repeatedly to upset the small boats with their tails. Now that they saw the people returning to the ship, they made savage rushes at them.

Diggens describes the scene:

I have seen pictures of fine people going back to burnt-out homes. So it was with the *Sarah Sands*. Her beautifully dressed women, who had been hurried into the boats with bare arms and necks and shoulders, came to the side again. But how different from the joyous, chatty crowd who were on the point of dining when the cry of "Fire" was raised!

Dresses were torn and crumpled, happy faces had become drawn and haggard, bright eyes were dull with weeping, and white, delicate skins were browned and blistered by the merciless tropical sun. These people filled with pity even those of us who had fought the flames, and in looking on their miseries we forgot our own.

Captain Castle did what he could to relieve them, and that was to order the sailmaker to get pieces of sail and canvas and make such coverings as he could for the scorched skins. And so coarse canvas was put upon the delicate finery.

There was no chance of luxury in such a floating shell, and all that ingenuity could do and decency provide was to rig a canvas screen to separate the ladies from the troops.

It is astounding to think what men can reconcile themselves to when they are the creatures of crippling circumstances. Here were we, who had been so cooped up in a small ship on a long run to India that we could scarcely move in our narrow quarters and close imprisonment; yet were we finding it possible to exist in half the space, huddled almost indiscriminately in an iron shell that only kept afloat by a miracle.

The after part of the transport was just a gutted mass of ironwork, open to the air and the sea. To look down into it was like being on the top of a building that has been destroyed by fire, with only bare girders and the gaunt walls visible.

The cabins had been blown out of the stern by the explosion; all the woodwork had long since vanished, and some of the iron had melted away. How could it be otherwise, with a heat which was so fierce that the very glass of the scuttles had melted, and hung like icicles now that it was cold! That fact alone will show you how intense was the heat—literally a furnace heat.

It is marvelous that the work of man could withstand such a consuming flame, and the survival of the ship was a noble tribute to the stoutness of her structure and the honesty of her build. She had been gutted by fire; now heavy seas struck her repeatedly, and as she rolled helplessly, our four enormous tanks of water, which were right below, were hurled from side to side, and we never knew when one or all of them would dash through the iron plating.

Strange and incongruous were the things we did after and resulting from the fire. Most striking of all, I think, was the erection of a tent—for the captain's use and other official purposes—on the iron wreckage where the stern cabins had been.

A tent on a floating wreck, in that wilderness of tropic sea! And below that tent was the torn, bent mass of ironwork, with the very propeller-shaft showing in the depths. Need a man be a sailor to understand our constant peril from shipping a sea, or even a mass of water which, in ordinary times, would only cause amusement?

The long fight was over and a glorious victory was won. But what was our prize? A mere hull, a ship half burnt away, and which was sound only forward of the mainmast. The smoke had gone and now only clouds of steam ascended and vanished in the air.

The *Sarah Sands* had now nearly twenty feet of water in her, and was so deep by the stern that every wave seemed as if it would overwhelm and sink her. We had only one sound mast, too, the mizzen having been burnt away and the main damaged.

We had saved the troopship from fire; now we had to preserve her from water, so we set to work again and patched her up. For a long time she was like a gigantic kettle aft, with the steam rising from her; but we pumped incessantly for two nights and a day. We rigged up a steering-gear, we covered over the rent sides with spars and canvas, and we got some sail up. That was after floundering and drifting helplessly about in a ship that had nothing to control her.

Then, suffering torture from thirst and hunger, because our fresh water and our provisions had been almost entirely destroyed, we struggled on for nine days more, when we got our gallant cripple into Port Louis in the Mauritius.

Until that time, from the hour we started from the Cape, we had seen neither ship nor land, so our deliverance was merciful indeed. If we had vanished, our fate would never have been known, because two or three bottles that were thrown overboard with messages were never picked up.

The irony of our fate was on us to the very last. A pilot came off and told us that he could not take us in till next morning, as ships were not allowed to enter in the darkness. No exception was made even for us, so for the first time since the fire the crazy screw was started slowly, and the *Sarah Sands* crawled off and on. She was nearly wrecked in the night on a reef, but in the morning she got in and we went ashore —some of us wrapped in newspapers to hide our nakedness.

For all the miseries we had suffered there was almost recompense in the things that were said about us, and the kindness which was shown. We had gone through that long-drawn time of peril from fire and sea and mutiny; we had saved our colours and our ship; we had held to our discipline and maintained the credit of our regiment, and we had not lost a life!

Can you wonder that of all the honours which the 54th has gained, there is none it holds dearer than this great triumph that was won upon the sea, and not the battlefield?

DON BRUNO'S TREASURE

The Don Bruno treasure was hidden on a lonely island more than one hundred years ago, but it was not until a mariner named Arthur Coleman entered the picture that there was any chance of recovering the hoard. A twenty-six-year-old Englishman in 1862, Coleman was chief officer aboard the steamer *City of Hobart,* then trading between Sydney, Hobart, and Melbourne, Australia.

In those days there were four mail steamers running between Sydney and Panama. According to Louis Becke, who was the first to hear of Coleman, the steamers were named *Rakaia, Mataura, Ruahine,* and *Kaikoura.* To be appointed to one of these liners was considered a distinction, and Coleman naturally felt elated when he was offered first officer's berth on the *Rakaia.* Bidding good-bye to the captain and officers of the *City of Hobart,* he went on board the mail steamer and immediately buckled down to learning and carrying out the duties of his new position.

Sixty days later the steamer was in Panama Harbor coaling for the return trip to Sydney, when suddenly Coleman was sent for by Macpherson, the line's Panama agent. A number of passengers for the Sydney steamer had just arrived by train from Aspinwall on the Atlantic side of the Isthmus, and the agent's offices were crowded.

As he was supervising the coaling of his ship, Coleman naturally was anxious to return to the vessel as soon as possible. Sending in his name by a clerk, he waited for five minutes or so with a fair amount of patience. The clerk had returned to say that Mr. Macpherson would see Mr. Coleman presently. At the end of ten minutes Coleman strode in again, and in sharp tones asked the clerk to tell Mr. Macpherson that he could not possibly remain another five minutes. A moment later Macpherson appeared, obviously ruffled and upset.

Macpherson, sent out to take charge of the Panama office, had been offensive and haughty during the passage over on Coleman's vessel. A measly-looking, insignificant creature with weak eyes, he was blessed with a wife who was the prettiest and sweetest little Scotswoman imaginable. Mrs. Macpherson had won the admiration of all on board, but her husband became heartily detested.

The moment Coleman saw him he endeavored to get through the crowd of people in the front office, who, seeing by his uniform that he was an officer of the *Rakaia,* made way for him.

"What is it, Mr. Macpherson?" asked Coleman.

"I'll not have you sending in messages for me to come out to you. I've important business to attend to."

Coleman was not a bad-tempered man, but the audible titter that ran round the office angered him almost beyond endurance.

"You sent for me on what you wrote was an important matter, you said. We have, as you know, only twelve hours in which to finish coaling. Tell me what it is. I have no time to waste here."

"How dare you talk to me that way?" screamed Macpherson. "My wife tells me that there is a watercolor picture belonging to me hanging up in your cabin. You'll just understand I'll have no nonsense about it, and so I sent for you to tell you so myself. Please send it to me directly."

"You infernal rascal!" shouted Coleman, and started for the agent. Macpherson attempted to get back into his private office. He was too late, for Coleman, whose temper had quite mastered him now, grabbed the agent by the collar.

"You damned miserable little beast! So you only sent for me to insult me? Well, you've done it. And now I'm going to take it out of you. Will any one lend me a cane?"

A Spaniard stepped forward and handed Coleman a light Malacca cane.

Quick as lightning Coleman pulled the little agent over his knees, and for a minute or so he belabored him. Then Coleman stood him up on his trembling legs again, and dragging the agent through the crowded front office to the street door, he gave Macpherson a kick, sending him flying headfirst out onto the pavement.

"By Jove, sir!" said a big fat man to Coleman as the mate stood glaring at the prostrate figure, "you'd better get aboard again. Served the cheeky little beast right. He won't be able to sit down for a month, but I think he's stunned."

Coleman proceeded on his way to the railway wharf, where a launch waited to take him over to Flamenco, the coaling pier.

Reaching the wharf, he suddenly heard hurried footsteps behind him. Four policemen grabbed him and he was taken to the Panama station. Half an hour later he was in a prison cell. This was all because, he thought to himself, he had hung Mrs. Macpherson's gift in his cabin instead of stowing it away in his chest, as she had desired. At dinnertime his captain came, and Coleman then learned he was in for serious trouble, for the news was bad. The agent was believed to be dying from a cracked skull, and of course Coleman would have to stay in prison.

The *Rakaia* sailed on schedule. Coleman lay in prison cursing his luck, hoping that it was not true about the fractured skull.

On the third day his jailers visited his cell. They told him that a gentleman wanted to see him. He had had plenty of visitors, principally Englishmen, from the consul to local clerks, all of whom had tried to cheer him up. Coleman had learned from the consul that little Macpherson, who was still alive but in very bad condition, meant to press the charge of attempted murder, and that the consul could do nothing for the prisoner.

Coleman, however, was glad to have another visitor. The moment he entered, the accused man recognized his guest as none other than the Spanish gentleman who had lent him the Malacca cane with which he had flogged the agent.

"Good-day, señor," he said, extending his hand. Then, in a low voice, he added in English, "What is this fellow's name?" pointing to the jailer then standing attentively in the corridor.

"Manuel."

Calling him over, the Spaniard put in his hand a gold piece. "Friend Manuel, I want to have half an hour's talk with Mr. Coleman here. I am interested in him. Every time I come here I will beg of you to accept a gold piece from me."

Manuel, grinning broadly, withdrew, and the Spaniard picked up a little stool. He placed it in front of Coleman, who sat on the cell bench.

"Señor Coleman, I desire to help you. In two days, if you will accept my assistance, you will be a free man. A little money goes a long way with those in power here. Do you understand?"

"Of course," replied Coleman. "I am afraid I'd almost do anything to get out of this mess."

"Be patient, please, and listen, and I will tell you why I desire to set you free. Answer me one question. Will you, when free, enter into my service for one year, at a salary to be named by you?"

"What is the nature of the employment?"

"I wish you to take the command of a vessel."

"Ah!" Coleman jumped to the conclusion that his visitor was connected with some revolutionary project. "I am not a naval officer; I am in the merchant's service."

"Precisely, I know that. But the service upon which you will be employed is one that does not need the training of a naval officer, and it is a perfectly honorable and legitimate adventure. Nevertheless, there may be danger. Does that satisfy you?"

"Perfectly."

"I was informed, Mr. Coleman, that you are a skillful navigator." Presently he looked up and caught the young seaman's eye. Smiling, he stroked his pointed beard and iron-gray mustache.

"You are wondering who I am. I should have been more courteous. My name is Pedro do Bustamente. Until six months ago I was a captain of infantry in the Spanish army in the garrison at Malaga. My father then died—in Cuenca. At his death certain property and documents came into my possession. I read the documents, and, placing faith in what I read, I sold the property, threw up my commission, took passage to Colon, and, had it not been for my witnessing your beating of the little man, would now be on my way to San Francisco or some other American seaport, where I could buy a small vessel for the purpose I have in view. But, señor, I like your face. I believe you to be an honorable man, and that a good fate designed our meeting. Good-bye for the present; in less than forty-eight hours you will be out of Panama."

"Well, that's queer!" muttered Coleman as he watched

Manuel bow his visitor out. "What can he want me for? Anyway, I'll go, if I don't get stabbed or garrotted here. I wonder if that poor little beggar I tossed on his head is really dying?"

But although Mr. Macpherson was then a long way from dying, both the English and American consuls knew that Coleman faced a long imprisonment, and Captain Pedro do Bustamente knew this too. Bustamente also knew, however, that by careful placement of gold coins the mate could be liberated, and so he lost no time.

That very night, at midnight, Coleman lay asleep. Manuel came to his cell, awakened him, and handed him a note. He read it aloud: "Put on the cloak and follow Manuel."

The jailer handed him a heavy woolen poncho. Coleman donned the garment and left his cell. In another minute the two men were out of the prison and walking quietly down the street. They continued in the same direction, until they came to the place where a man was waiting, holding three mules. The man was Bustamente. Without a word, all three mounted and jogged quietly along, following the coastline northward. At daylight they drew up beside a small roadside inn, or fonda.

"Let us halt and get some breakfast," said Bustamente. "These people here are expecting us. I assure you that there is no fear of any pursuit—that is, if money has any virtue."

As they ate, Bustamente explained that he had studied English in England, having for many years been in the suite of the Spanish minister in London.

All that day they rode northward. By nightfall they entered a little seaport town on the shore of Parita Bay. Here Manuel left them, happy with $350 in gold he then received. Ten hours later they were on board the American steamer *Nebraska* bound to San Francisco, for Bustamente had arranged with the captain of the steamer to call for them on her way along the coast.

As the clumsy old side-wheeler steamed off the shores of Costa Rica, the Spaniard and Coleman sat in their deck cabin. Presently Bustamente put his hand in his breast pocket and pulled out a bundle of papers.

"Now, my friend, I can talk. I think you will find my story interesting."

Indeed it was not only interesting but fascinating. The remarkable tale began in 1850. His father, Bruno do Bustamente, a Spaniard by birth, was the richest merchant at Mazatlán, on the coast of Mexico, and traded largely with the East. The governor of the province of Durango, whose hostility he had incurred, had him imprisoned on a trumped-up charge, and from that day he was the prey of the Mexican authorities, who sought to subject him to a continuous process of extortion and blackmail.

Bruno's wife was a Mexican lady of San Blas, and they had two children, a son and daughter. The son, Pedro, he had sent to Spain to enter the army.

Upon regaining his freedom and paying a fine of $5,000 to the governor of Durango, Bruno determined to leave Mexico and return to Spain. About this time his wife died. He turned his holdings into money, realized upon his various estates, and sold all his vessels but one, a brigantine of 120 tons named the *Bueno Esperanza*. The captain of this vessel was an American named Devine, in whom he had the most implicit confidence.

At the time there was but little gold coin in use in that part of Mexico, and Bruno had in many cases to take payment in silver Mexican dollars for the properties he had sold. Of these silver dollars he had received something like ninety thousand, in addition to sixty-five thousand dollars in gold. Secured in bags made of green hide, the money was carried from day to day on board the *Bueno Esperanza*.

Fearing every moment that he would be detained and his fortune seized by the Mexican authorities, the Don announced that he was dispatching the brig on one of her usual voyages to San Blas. He explained that his daughter, Engracia, was going there also to visit her mother's relatives. Accompanied by her nurse, the little girl went on board. When the brig finally sailed, Don Bruno had the satisfaction of seeing her safe on board. The treasure was still unmolested. But instead of San Blas, the *Bueno Esperanza* was bound to Manilla,* in the Philippine Islands, where Devine was to await the arrival of his master.

A month went by. Don Bruno, having disposed of the remainder of the property, followed them in an American trading schooner he had chartered for the purpose. After a quick passage he arrived safely at Manilla. There, to his dismay and grief, he learned that nothing had been seen of the *Bueno Esperanza* which should have reached port a month before him.

The days went by and there was no news at all. Month after month elapsed. Finally, the distracted merchant, now broken in health and fortune, returned to end his days in his native town of Cuenca, Spain. His death there was very sudden. His son Pedro learned from the old housekeeper that the death occurred on the same day on which he had received a letter which bore a foreign postmark. Upon reading the letter he had become terribly agitated.

After telling his housekeeper that he desired to write to his son in Malaga, she left him, and upon returning a quarter of an hour afterward, she found him dead with his head upon the table. Under his stiff hand was a sheet of paper, on which were scrawled a few words to his son. Death had taken him too quickly to write more, and beside it lay the letter bearing the foreign postmark.

These were given to Captain Bustamente as soon as he reached the house a few days later.

* In 1862 the name of the city was spelled Manilla rather than Manila.

Coleman listened carefully as the Spaniard unreeled the astounding account of his father's adventures. Pedro then picked up a paper.

"Here are my father's last words," said the Spaniard. Coleman read:

"The money will be there. Seek for it. I command you in the name of the Holy Virgin to give Christian burial to the bones of your sister. I pray . . ."

The remaining two or three lines were so confused they could not be understood. Bustamente continued his story.

"And now read this—the letter he received an hour before his death. It is in English, and is dated just one year and two months ago. The enclosure is in Spanish."

Ship *Sadie Wilmot,*
New Bedford U.S.A.,
6th March, 1861.

Mr. Bruno Do Bustamente
Cuenca, Spain.

Dear Sir;—The ship *Sadie Wilmot,* of which I am master, while cruising for sperm whales between Mindanao in the Philippines and the Pelews, on the 14th August, 1860, picked up a ship's boat containing the dead bodies of five persons, who had evidently died from thirst and starvation. In a tin box found in the boat was the enclosed letter to you, and the sum of one thousand dollars in Mexican gold coin. If you can establish a claim to this I am prepared to forward same, less charges. My second mate, who is a native of the Azores, read the letter addressed to you. I believe that the island mentioned is uninhabited. I was too far to the westward when the boat was found to go back and see if any of the crew had remained there. Please reply to A. Wilmot, New Bedford.

Yours truly,
Amos Wilmot

Coleman handed him back the letter, and then Bustamente slowly unfolded a single sheet of paper, written upon in pencil. On the top of the sheet was written in English:

In case of my death I ask that this may be sent to Don Bruno do Bustamente, Cuenca, Spain, or to his son Pedro, at Malaga.

The following was written in Spanish:

Wrecked on an uninhabited island in lat. 7° 29′ N. long. 160° 42′ E. Six of the crew drowned, also owner's child, Engracia Bustamente, and her nurse. The body of the former was buried at a spot above high-water mark, about 300 yards from a large round knob of rock, covered with vines on the eastern point and bearing E. by N. from the grave. No provisions were saved except some jerked beef, packed in hide bags. Were four months on the island. Left there July 3rd, in open boat, to try and reach Manilla.

Devine.

With flashing eyes the Spaniard sprang to his feet and placed his hands on Coleman's shoulders.

"Ah, that brave man, that Devine! Cannot your understand? These words of his were written so that my father, if ever they came to his hand, would know that the treasure had been saved and hidden. 'The jerked beef in hide bags.' The money was in hide bags! And I think that instead of my poor sister being buried on the spot he speaks of, there we will find it."

He walked up and down the cabin quickly.

"And then, see how careful he has been to avoid telling the name of the brigantine, where she was from and where bound to. He knew that my father would return to Spain after he had given up all hope of the *Bueno Esperanza;* that in Cuenca, his birthplace, he would spend the rest of his days. He feared to say more. My good friend, I am certain that unless my father spoke of those bags of bullock-hide to people in Manilla, not a living soul but you and I know that the brig carried a hundred and fifty thousand dollars in gold and silver. And we will go to this island and get them."

Their course of action was soon decided upon. By the sale of the little property he had inherited from Don Bruno his son had realized nearly a thousand pounds. Out of this he had paid nearly two hundred pounds, the greater part of which had gone for Coleman's escape. With something like eight hundred pounds, or four thousand dollars, he and Coleman landed in San Francisco.

A week afterward they chartered a small fore-and-aft vessel of fifty tons, the *Marion Price,* for five hundred dollars a month, provisioned her for six months, and with three Hawaiian natives for a crew, sailed out of the Golden Gate for the island.

On the twenty-seventh day out the little *Marion Price* passed the first of the Caroline group, a chain of low, sandy atolls, covered densely with coconuts. That night Coleman hove to. If the position of the island they sought was given correctly in Devine's account of the wreck they were not more than forty miles to the eastward of it.

At daylight Coleman stood away to the westward and sent one of the Hawaiians up aloft. While he and Bustamente were at breakfast they heard the cry of "Land, ho!"

The breeze was steady. At eleven o'clock the *Price* was within a mile of their objective, and the two men scanned the strange island with interest.

Two miles in circumference, it was of considerable height for its size. On three sides gray coral cliffs rose from the surf that lashed and foamed at their base. Only on the lee side was the island protected by a fringing reef. In some places the wall of cliffs sank to perhaps fifty or sixty feet, in others it rose to nearly two hundred or more, but preserved the same grim and savage monotony of appearance. Broken, jagged pinnacles of coral were concealed by a dense, impenetrable growth of short, stunted scrub and masses of vine and creepers. Here and there these creepers had grown over the face of the cliff itself, and hung down over the surf, resembling monstrous carpets of green and yellow. Rocky pinnacles above them resembled neatly trimmed pine trees.

"Small hope for a man if a ship strikes here," said Coleman with an involuntary shudder, looking at the wild breakers roaring in. "Ah, we're opening up the south point now, and there's a long reef running out there. Get aloft, one of you fellows, and see if there is a break in it anywhere."

As the schooner stood out again they got a better view of the island, and could see that although on the weather side a good landing was impossible, it sloped gradually to the westward. Suddenly there was a shout from aloft.

"I see tops of coconut trees over other trees. Now there is smooth water, sir; I see beach and passage, too."

Rounding the point of the long stretch of reef, Coleman hauled up and ran close in again. Suddenly his arm was seized by the Spaniard.

"Look!" and Pedro pointed to the shore.

On the eastern point of the island, there stood in bold relief a huge, round boulder, flattened at the apex, but perfect in the symmetry of its outlines and covered with vines!

The two men grasped each other's hands in silence, for the rock was the same spoken of by Devine. Debris from the wreck littered the shore around it.

Another half hour and Coleman had let go his anchor in

five fathoms, on a white, sandy bottom. Taking one native, he and his friend lowered the boat and pulled toward the beach.

When they landed on the shore and studied the debris from the wrecked *Bueno Esperanza,* they decided that the long, grinding reef just offshore was the one which had caught the brigantine in its fatal grasp. The first objects they saw were some spars, then a mast and finally a broken topsail yard, the ends of which were protruding from a heaped-up pile of loose coral slabs.

Clambering over the stony bank, soon they came across a grove of coconuts, beneath which were the ruins of a deck-house and a quantity of planking, barrels, ironwork, and other material saved from the brigantine. There for two years the wreckage had lain undisturbed, blistering and cracking under the rays of a tropical sun, ever since the unfortunates who had lived in the deckhouse had left its shelter to die of the horrors of thirst in a small open boat.

Fifty feet or so from the rotting, tumbledown deckhouse they found the rude grave of the little Spanish child. It was a square structure of coral slab, over which the vines had crept and bound themselves together.

Pedro do Bustamente, baring his head, knelt for a moment and prayed for the soul of the little sister he had not seen since they had played together in the days of his childhood.

Then he motioned to the Hawaiian sailor to cut away the binding creepers from the stones.

In a few minutes this was done. The three men rapidly removed the small slabs of loose coral. The coffin of the little girl had been constructed very solidly, and as a protection from decay had been covered with copper taken from the wreck.

After carefully lifting it out, Coleman, at the Spaniard's request, made an examination of the bottom of the grave. He was soon satisfied that it had contained nothing else but that which they had taken from it.

To Coleman's surprise Pedro showed no disappointment and asked him in quiet tones if he would help him carry the coffin to the boat.

This was done, and they returned to the schooner. Placing the coffin on the cabin table and covering it with a flag, the two men came on deck again.

"My friend," said the Spaniard, "now that my duty is done, let us get the treasure."

"Where shall we look for it?"

"There," said Pedro, pointing to the great rock outlined clearly before them, "three hundred yards east by north from the grave!"

Taking with them the three Hawaiians, who were provided with long, heavy knives to cut through the scrub, they returned to the shore.

It took then some time to clear a path, but at last they stood at the foot of the huge boulder. A thorough examination revealed nothing in the way of a cave or hollow anywhere about the foot or sides.

Pulling themselves up by the vines, they clambered to the top. Here they discovered that the flattened summit of the rock had in reality a large depression in the center, over which the creepers had grown and formed a thick network.

Standing in the center they found that, although the bed of vines sank under their feet, there was still a hollow space between them and the bottom. The Hawaiians climbed up and set to work slashing the vines around the edge of the miniature crater with their knives.

Then the five men, hauling on the heavy mass, dragged it to the edge, and tumbled it over the side. In great excitement Bustamente jumped down into the hollow, sinking up to his knees in the mass of dead leaves and debris from the vines.

In a moment he plunged his hands into the debris and groped about. Then he looked up.

"It is here!"

Coleman and a native sprang down after him. The moment Coleman's feet touched the bottom Pedro, in wild enthusiasm, threw his arms around his comrade, embracing him.

Now came the time to clear away the dead leaves and vines. There was barely standing room in which to work. With neither bags nor baskets, the sailors took off their shirts and threw them down to Pedro and Coleman, who quickly filled them with debris and then passed them up. As they worked they could feel under their feet the rotted hide bags coming apart under their weight. As the last load of rubbish was collected they dragged up a piece of hide bagging, clinging to the inside of which were some Mexican sun dollars, stained and discolored.

Tearing away the uppermost side of the rotting bags of hide, they found at their feet the lost treasure of Bruno do Bustamente, just as his faithful captain had placed it in the hollow rock two years before. So rotten and decayed were the topmost layer of bags, that the contents, under the weight of their bodies, had spread out and formed a thick and even surface of silver coins, which hid from view the bags beneath.

For an hour the men worked collecting the loose Mexican dollars. Then two sailors were sent back to the schooner for canvas, needles, palms, and twine. Meanwhile Coleman clambered to the top again. The others passed up handful after handful of money from the rocky cavity.

As soon as the sailors returned, the five men set to work at the canvas, cutting it up and shaping it into rough bags, into which the loose coin was placed and sewn up.

The rest of the bags had not gone to pieces, and with careful handling, were taken out. Then the men came to eight smaller packages, which proved to be wooden boxes covered with hide. Taking a hatchet, Bustamente knocked the outside covering off one, and then pried open the lid. It contained gold.

They lifted out the eight boxes, placing them on the rock beside the bags.

Then, satsifying themselves that all the treasure had been found, they had a good meal. Each man then picked up a box or bag. They made their way in single file back to the beach, returned again and again till the last load had been brought down and put in the boat. Ten minutes later they reached the schooner. Finally all the gold and silver was stored in the cabin of the *Marion Price*.

It was dark before their work was finished. Pedro and Coleman then went below to the cabin, which indeed presented an unusual scene. Around them lay bags and boxes of gold and silver, with the light from the lamp falling upon the flag-covered coffin of the Spanish girl.

"Poor little one," murmured Pedro do Bustamente, placing his hand tenderly on the flag, "thou shalt rest beside our father in Spain."

That night they opened the boxes of gold and counted the money. In one they found a paper written by Devine, which gave a detailed account of the wreck of the *Bueno Esperanza*. It concluded by saying that he had opened that box and had taken from it a thousand dollars, for it was his intention to leave the island and endeavor to reach Manilla, where he expected to find Don Bruno awaiting him. They could then charter a vessel and return to the island for the treasure.

As Coleman surmised, the *Bueno Esperanza* had run ashore at night on the long horn of reef stretching out from the south point. The sea had been fairly smooth at the time, but the brigantine ground heavily on the coral. Seeing no hope of floating her, Devine and his crew proceeded to save all they could. The treasure was safely landed at daylight. Then the sea began to rise, and battered the brigantine, which commenced to break up. The sailors had remained on the vessel too long, however, for in returning to shore both boats were capsized by a huge sea. Six men drowned from the mate's boat, while the Mexican nurse and the little Engracia, both of whom were in the captain's boat, were frightfully injured by the coral. They died the next day. The nurse was buried on the beach, and the little girl, who lingered longer, in the grove of palms.

After reading this sorrowful record the two men proceeded to open and count the bags of silver. The treasure amounted to ninety-three thousand Mexican and Spanish dollars, and, with the gold, the total was $154,000. Thus all except the thousand dollars taken by Devine was recovered.

The next morning Bustamente called the three Hawaiians aft and told them that on the arrival of the schooner at Manilla he would give them five hundred dollars each over and above their wages; but he asked them to swear secrecy.

Kahola, a huge broad-shouldered native from the island of Oahu, looked intently into the Spaniard's face. Then, bidding his fellow countrymen stand back, he spoke slowly and carefully.

"What I swear, those two men swear too. If you please, sir, you wait till I get something."

He walked forward and disappeared below, returning in a minute or two with a book whose size was only surpassed by its dirty appearance.

"This is our Bible," said Kahola. "We swear to keep your secret, but you also swear the money is really yours."

Standing beside Bustamente, the Hawaiian beckoned to the two others to stand beside him, and held out the book to the Spaniard.

"All right, sir, now. You go ahead and swear us here on our Bible."

The Spaniard nodded gravely, and took off his cap. The Hawaiians already held their battered hats under their arms, which were crossed over their broad and naked chests. With their eyes fixed upon his face, they waited. The Spaniard raised the book.

"Will you, Kahola, and you, Liho, and you, Bob, swear to me, Pedro do Bustamente, to speak to no man about the money on board this ship until you return to your own country, or till such time as I and Captain Coleman shall fix upon?"

"We do," answered Kahola.

"Now what would you have me swear, Kahola?" said Bustamente.

"Me and my countrymen like you swear, sir, on this good book, that this money belong to you."

The Spaniard raised the book to his lips. "On this book, which is the Word of God, and by the body of my dead sister, who lies in her coffin beneath us, I swear to you Kahola, and you, Liho, and you, Bob, that the money we have taken is mine. It was once my father's. He is dead, but before he died he told me where to seek for it."

"Good," said Kahola, and he reached out his brawny hand for the book, and then added, in Hawaiian, "What is the father's shall be the son's, for that is the law of God and the law of man."

The big sailor then swore the oath.

"I, Kahola, will tell no man one word about the money. Suppose I tell something, I hope God kill me dead, and give me damn bad luck."

Liho and Bob repeated the same words, and then with smiling faces they shook hands with Bustamente and Coleman. The ceremony ended, the Hawaiians turned to their regular duties.

By noon the island had sunk to a purple speck on the horizon, and Pedro and Coleman, with joy in their hearts, were sitting on the deck.

"My dear comrade," said Pedro, placing his hand affectionately on Coleman's shoulder, "you must—you *shall* do as I wish. Both you and I are alone in the world. Let us be comrades always. See now, it was so intended by God for us to meet, and therefore fifty thousand dollars of the money is thine; that will leave me plenty!"

Coleman began to remonstrate, but Pedro placed his hand on his mouth. "But that I had found such a true man, I may have never succeeded in finding it."

And this is the true story of the finding of the lost treasure of Don Bruno do Bustamente, as related to marine historian Louis Becke a few years before the turn of the present century.

11

THE AUCKLAND ISLES

One of the most astounding tales in maritime history is that of two ships, the *Grafton* and the *Invercauld*, wrecked the same year at the Auckland Isles in the South Pacific only a few miles apart. As the months went by, survivors from both ships came within a short distance of each other while they were marooned, but they never knew it. Not until one party was leaving the island for good did they discover a dead man who was probably from the other crew.

A mystery exists concerning a wisp of smoke evidently from a campfire which Captain Thomas Musgrave of the *Grafton* noticed one day. Although it was thought later by newsmen that the smoke was probably from a fire started by the other party, my studies of the accounts of each group indicate that the survivors of the *Invercauld* had left the island months before Captain Musgrave saw the smoke.

Without question, few more vivid accounts involving shipwreck and disaster at sea have ever been written than the journals in which Captain Musgrave recorded the wreck of his beloved ship, *Grafton*, and his subsequent existence on the far-flung Auckland Isles.

The *Grafton,* under the command of Captain Musgrave, sailed from Sydney, Australia, for the South Sea Islands on November 12, 1863. Thomas Musgrave tells the story of his experiences with the simplicity and directness of a sailor. He records, in interesting fashion the weather, the thermometer's ups and downs, and barometric pressures. His comments on his own strange life are also written in a style which smacks of the sea. The traits of the sea lions and the unusually tame birds are likewise effectively handled in his island journals.

By studying Musgrave's account with his excellent description of the islands and of his experiences a century earlier, I was able to step mentally into the position of being one of the castaways on this uninhabited island. The story begins in detail late in December, when the *Grafton* was in the general vicinity of the Auckland Islands.

On Thursday, December 31, 1863, shortly after the sun crossed the meridian, it came on to blow a gale. Immediately Captain Musgrave ordered sail reduced to close-reefed topsail, foresail, and foretop mainstaysail. What the captain called a "dangerous, confused sea" began to run and broke on board in all directions. To make matters worse, a thick fog set in with drizzling rain.

By six o'clock that night, although the sea began to run in more regular fashion, the vessel was still straining heavily. At nine o'clock in the morning Auckland Island was sighted.

"As the wind will not permit me to weather the island, I have determined to go under its lee, and if possible, cast anchor in 'Sarah's Bosom,' " wrote Captain Musgrave.

On New Year's Day at noon, Auckland Island was about eight miles away. At three o'clock that afternoon, the *Grafton* entered the harbor which Captain Musgrave thought was named Sarah's Bosom, but actually was Carnley's Harbor.

The schooner beat in, but since the sailors could find no bottom at twenty fathoms, the *Grafton* kept under weigh all night. Great numbers of seals appeared in all directions and began to play around the vessel like porpoises.

At six o'clock on New Year's Day, 1864, they put the boat out to look for an anchorage but found none. Two hours later a strong breeze blew up from the northwest, which soon devel[0]pd into a gale. The captain ordered both anchors put over in six fathoms of water close to shore. "I consider her in a rather dangerous position, as there is hardly room for her to swing clear of the rocks, should the wind come from the S.W.," he wrote.

On Saturday, the next day, the gale blew heavily and a swell began to run. "The ship has been jerking and straining at her chains all day, and I expected them to part every moment."

Then in a heavy squall, the starboard chain parted and the other anchor began to drag. Finally she was brought up, her stern in a quarter less two fathoms * about half a cable's length from the shore.

There were five men aboard—Captain Musgrave; Raynal, the French mate; and three sailors. The fierce gale which drove the *Grafton* on a rock threw her broadsides on the beach, enabling the crew to land in safety and to carry off their scant stock of provisions. The mainsail and gaff were brought on shore and made into a tent.

The survivors had just finished setting up quarters on the island when a furious hurricane hit which lasted a full week. During this period they slept in the shelter of the tent every night, but on the wet ground.

As the days went by the five men soon became conscious of their neighbors, the seals. The trusting animals paid them frequent visits, thus bringing fresh meat up to the very door of their tent. Let us read from the Musgrave journal:

* Roughly ten and a half feet.

⚓

Sunday, January 3, 1864 . . . Today is also a very fine day, with a moderate N.W. breeze. Last Monday we went on board the wreck, and got all the boards we could muster to make a floor in the tent, as we had all got severe colds from lying on the wet ground. We also unbent the sails, and sent down all the yards and topmasts, and are using them for building a house, as in all probability we shall have to remain here all next winter; and if we want to preserve life, we must have shelter. We have all worked very hard, and although it has been so wet we have succeeded in getting up the frame of the house. We live chiefly on seal meat, as we have to be very frugal with our own little stock; we kill them at the door of the tent as we require them. . . .

The vessel leaves her bones here, and God only knows whether we are all to leave our bones here also. And what is to become of my poor unprovided-for family? It drives me mad to think of it. I can write no more.

᚛

Fearing that the seals would eventually break into the tent, the captain shot several one night, and the others took the hint; afterward they kept at a respectful distance. Musgrave tells us that a young seal is delicious, tasting exactly like lamb.

One day while crossing the bay the survivors were attacked by a bull seal which swam furiously toward their boat. As it put its head over the stern, with its mouth wide open, the captain fired directly down the bull seal's throat. His "head flew in all directions," and his body sank like a stone.

Soon after this the captain saw two great seals fighting. There were hundreds of others watching the battle, the shores and the water literally swarming with them. The tiger seals kept at one side of the harbor and the black seals at the other. In this instance, one from each army had met and were heatedly engaged in battle when Captain Musgrave first noticed them.

Fighting as ferociously as dogs, the participants made no noise at all, tearing each other almost to pieces with their large tusks. Often after a fight of this kind, the seals suffer horribly. Musgrave noticed one in particular with his neck and back lacerated in fearful fashion. Large pieces of hide and flesh were torn off, several a foot long and four or five inches wide. When the sailors walked up to him, the seal refused to budge, looking at the mariners "with all possible coolness and unconcern."

Several kinds of birds on the island were identified by the sailors, two of them sweet singers. They also saw a green parrot and a robin which were so tame that anyone could catch them by stretching out his hand. The robins were frequent visitors to the tent, chirping cheerily to the castaways.

The castaways' tent was actually a "beastly place." The blowflies soon covered their blankets and clothes, making everything disgusting. Mosquitoes tormented them in the daytime but for some reason did not disturb them at night. Soon the men found that the tent was unbearable and started to build a house. They had saved a hammer, an ax, an adz, and a gimlet from the wreck, but these were all the tools they had.

By the time the house was finished they had erected a flagpole high on a promontory some distance away. From it they flew a large canvas bag where it might attract the attention of vessels at sea. Then they tied a bottle to it with a note inside, directing any person who found it to the house where he could discover the survivors of the *Grafton*.

One day the captain decided to climb a neighboring mountain to survey the terrain, but when he got there he found it very discouraging. In every direction the prospects of travel were almost impossible. The land was either swampy, boggy, or impenetrable. Actually during the year and a half that Musgrave remained on the island, he never went farther than a few miles, either by boat or on foot, from the scene of the wreck, probably because his first excursion nearly proved fatal to him.

On this occasion the captain chased a seal into the under-brush for about two miles. Unfortunately, his gun had been loaded for two days, so that his powder had become damp. After he snapped two or three caps, one barrel fired. Entering the seal's neck, the ball came out between the creature's shoulders. Indifferent to such a trifle, the seal continued his escape. The captain tried again; once more the cap merely snapped. Disgusted, Musgrave placed the butt of the gun at his feet and started to unload it. Off it went, the ball passing through the rim of his hat. Captain Musgrave gave up and returned to the house, visibly shaken by his narrow escape. He rarely went into the brush again.

Their residence, which they named Epigwaitt House, was slowly built some distance north of what came to be called Musgrave Peninsula. After weeks of laborious efforts, the men finally finished the shelter. It was twenty-four feet by sixteen with walls seven feet high, and included a chimney built of stone, eight feet by five. The corner posts and center posts, the wall plates and ridgepoles, were spars from the ship. The walls were made of brush timber, which, although crooked from the force of frequent hurricanes, were placed up and down and close together.

As the timber was crooked, letting in air and snow, it was decided to thatch the whole house, sides and top, for further protection. The canvas, which they originally used, admitted a great deal of wind, and as there was a gale almost constantly

blowing, the shelter at first was far from ideal. Boards covered
the floor, a good door hung at the entrance, and two small
squares of glass taken from the cabin of the wreck made a
window.

The castaways had stretchers to sleep on, six feet from the
floor. A large dining table, seven feet by three, stood in the
center of the house with benches placed on each side. The
captain saw to it that he retained his position of leadership.
"I sat not on the benches, but on a keg, at the head."

On Sunday, March 27, 1864, Musgrave wrote as follows:

The roof remains covered with canvas. Today I went in
the boat up the harbour; I have not been there before. This
harbour is rather narrow, but quite broad enough for any
ship to work up. It is about half a mile wide in the narrowest
place, which is about the entrance, and in some places it is
about one and a half miles wide. I find that this is a proper
place to anchor a vessel in; it is well sheltered from the pre-
vailing winds, and there appears to be none of those sudden
gusts of wind which are so frequent and dangerous in this part
of the harbour.

There are several streams of beautiful water emptying into
the bay; two of them are the largest I have yet found in any
part of the islands. We tried fishing, but unsuccessfully. We
killed one seal and a number of widgeons,* and then returned
home. We did not see any seals on shore, but we saw great
numbers in the water. I suppose, as it was fine day, they were
all out fishing.

There must be a great number of fish in these harbours to
supply so many seals, but we have not yet found out how to

* Several varieties of wild duck.

catch them. All the fish we have got as yet we have picked up amongst the seaweed and stones on the beach at low water.

During the last day or two all the snow has disappeared from the mountains. I hope we shall have some fine weather yet before the winter sets in. The barometer is very high today, 30.20; and the thermometer 47° in the shade. I have found another small bottle of black ink, so I shall use it while it lasts; for I see that the seals' blood fades away very much.

↩

Regardless of his being the captain whom the men treated in an obedient and respectful manner, Musgrave found that a spirit of independence was asserting itself before the first month was over.

⚓

It is true I no longer hold any command over them, but I share everything that has been saved from the wreck in common with them, and I have worked as hard as any of them in trying to make them comfortable, and I think gratitude ought to prompt them to still continue willing and obedient. But you might as well look for the grace of God in a highwayman's log-book as gratitude in a sailor; this is a well known fact.

↩

Nevertheless, when the captain treated his men as human beings, he found no cause to complain. He decided to teach school in the evenings and to read prayers and the scriptures, expounding the text to the best of his ability. Some of his men could not read, but they were willing to try, and he taught them. They learned eagerly and rapidly. Especially fond of hearing the Bible, they eventually gave up swearing, if we are to believe the captain.

One day they visited a small island in the harbor. Because of its peculiar shape they named it Figure-of-Eight Island.

⚓

We landed on the island and found three mobs of seals asleep. There were from thirty to forty in each mob, and there were a great many very young calves among them. These we wanted to get without killing our old ones. I had only two men with me; so we took our clubs, and each of us took a mob, and I suppose in ten seconds we had knocked down ten calves from two to three months old, and one two-year-old seal. We had to go right in among them, and although they woke up, we were so quick about the job that they stared at us in confusion for a moment, and then by a simultaneous movement rushed toward the water.

We could have got more, but one of the men was at this moment attacked by the only remaining one, which was a tremendous large bull—the largest tiger seal I have seen—and he fought like a tiger. We immediately rushed to the rescue; the poor fellow was obliged to take to a tree till we came up, when all three set on to the seal. And he showed fight bravely. It was as long as ten minutes before we proved ourselves conquerors; and we would have been quite willing to get out of his way, but he would not give us a chance. We were in a thick bush, so that he had a decided advantage. However, we left him, as he was too big for us to attend to when we had so many little ones to look after. This was the greatest piece of excitement I have had for a long time.

↩

The diet was more varied than might have been expected.
Besides feeding on seal meat, the men shot a number of
widgeons and shags, and gathered mussels and limpets among
the rocks. They found roots which were edible, if not wholly
delicious. They took turns at cooking, but it was the Frenchman who won the "honors of the kitchen."

"He very frequently gave us four courses at a meal. (Anyone might wonder where we got anything to make four
courses of; but we are like the shell-fish—we get the most at
spring-tides.) One would be stewed or roasted seal, fried liver,
fish and mussels."

Fish they could not catch at first, as they had neither tackle
nor nets; but necessity soon taught them to devise ways and
means for ensnaring them, and before long they had daily and
ample supplies. They also succeeded in making a sort of root
beer, which they found preferable to water in taste. But after
a time they were obliged to abandon it, for although it was
sweet in the mouth it was bitter elsewhere. The same root was
used for food, fried in seal's oil.

Further excerpts of Captain Musgrave's journal follow:

⚓

Sunday, March 13, 1864. My heart beats fast tonight as
I sit down to write, somewhat similar to what it might do if
I was about writing a love letter. I know that many a bitter
tear has been shed for me by this time, and most likely today,
as this is the end of another dreary month since I left those I
loved so much; and how many more must pass, or how they
will pass them until we meet again, or whether we shall ever
meet again on earth—Heaven only knows. These thoughts,

and such as these, which now prey continually on my mind, are maddening. I feel as if I was gradually consumed by an inward fire. I strive, by occupying my hands as much as possible, to dispel these sad feelings; but it is utterly impossible. A melancholy is getting hold of me; I am getting as thin as a lantern, and some disordered fluttering and heavy beating of the heart, which causes a faintness, is troubling me. I have felt this before, but only on one particular occasion, and that is some time ago. Were it not for the hope that I shall yet again be of service to my family, I think my spirit, if not my health, would break down; although under my present afflictions my continual prayer is that God may soon deliver me out of them.

Sunday, April 3, 1864 . . . On Monday last we went to Figure-of-Eight Island to get some young meat. We found the young seals as numerous as ever, if not more so; and this time they would not take to water at all. We were obliged to go right in amongst them, and they showed fight bravely. However, we got three young ones without killing any old ones.

While on the island we found a place where some party had camped at some time. There is no doubt but that they were killing seals, as we found a number of bricks, which no doubt had been used for their try works. There had been two tents pitched, and from the appearance of the ground where they had their fire, I should judge that they remained about a week. The ground all over these islands, except on the mountains, is of a turfy nature, and burns away whenever a fire is made; it is by this means that I judge from the place where the fire has been how long they have remained. How long it is since they were here I am unable to conjecture, but it is evident that ships visit this harbour sometimes; very probably it has been a whaler come in for wood or water, and finding the seals so numerous has taken a few. I am delighted to see even this sign of ships coming here; there is no doubt but we shall be released from our bondage some time—perhaps sooner than we expect. May it please God for it to be so! We sailed all round one of the heads of this harbour, taking soundings all the way, and I find anchorage in 10 and 11 fathoms; but there is an excellent anchorage in 15 fathoms, between Figure-of-Eight Island and Round Point.

↩

On May 10, his thirty-second birthday, Captain Musgrave pledged his mother by drinking a glass of beer made from a tree root.

On June 20 he speaks of the seals appearing on shore at night to sleep, at which time his men could kill them. He hiked across that afternoon to Signal Point where the signal board was found intact. He also mentions having nearly exhausted the supply of fish and mussels near their headquarters. We continue with his words:

⚓

Yesterday we all (excepting the cook) went on to the mountains to the north, taking the same track up that I took on the 24th January. We traveled on until we reached the top of a mountain which is situated about the centre of the island, and is, I think, the highest part of the land. From here we had a full view of the whole group. The south island, as I noticed on the 13th January, is scarcely disconnected, and one to the extreme north is at some distance from the mainland—perhaps six miles, and it may be about six miles in circumference. The whole extent of the group from north to south I judge to be 30 or 35 miles, and about fifteen miles east and west at the widest part.

The western shore is high and bold, particularly the southern end, carrying almost a straight line N.N.E., and with one or two small islets (perhaps there are more; I saw two) off the middle of the island, but close to it.

Sunday, July 24, 1864. We have heard the dogs barking several times during the last week, but we have not seen them. We frequently see their tracks in the woods, but not near the house. I think it very strange that they don't; for I feel convinced that these precise dogs have been left here by some one, for, had male and female been left, there would have been more now.

Sunday, July 31, 1864 . . . I think I have never described our precise mode of dragging out this miserable existence, for I cannot call it living. Breakfast—Seal stewed down to soup, fried roots, boiled seal, or roast ditto, with water. Dinner— Ditto ditto. Supper—Ditto ditto. This repeated twenty-one times per week. Mussels or fish are now quite a rarity; we have not been able to get either for some time. The man who killed the seal today had been fishing nearly all day, and had caught one small fish. The men have stood it bravely thus far, but it grieves me unspeakably to hear them wishing for things which they cannot get. I heard one just now wishing he had but a bucket of potato peelings!

Sunday, August 28, 1864 . . . And now, as my book is full, I shall continue my journal page 138 in another book. The barometer has been about 29.50 all the week, and is now rising, 29.80. Thermometer at noon 40°.

Sarah's Bosom. Sunday, September 4, 1864. It is now eight months since I had the misfortune to be cast away on this miserable island.

I have employed myself all the week in working at our new place, and I am going to much more trouble than is absolutely necessary, so as to divert my mind as much as possible from melancholy thoughts and forebodings. To judge by the pains I am taking with it, any one would suppose that we intended to pass the remainder of our days here, which may be the case; but if life and health are spared me, I shall not remain here another twelve months, if I go to sea in a boat and drown like a rat—which would be the most probable result—which mode of getting out of this world could not be termed suicide; although by those who are aware of the risk in so doing it might be considered systematic self-destruction, which I hope I shall not have occasion to adopt.

⊄

During the middle of September the seals started to vanish, and it was agreed that a trip of twelve miles to the "northern arm" for seals should soon be attempted.

⚓

      Sunday, October 23, 1864 . . . On Tuesday morning, Raynal and I set off at five o'clock in the morning to go on to the mountains to the northward and have a look round. The night had been beautifully fine and clear, and when we started there was not a cloud in the sky, and scarcely a breath of wind. A finer morning could not have been, but before we arrived at the top clouds rose from the westward and passed rapidly over, till the whole sky was covered, and a mist began to settle on the land, which soon became a dense fog, with heavy rain.

    It continued for several hours, and we were very glad that we had not got to the top, and made our way back again as quickly as possible. It would be exceedingly dangerous to be caught on the top of these mountains in one of those thick fogs; for sometimes you cannot see two yards before you, so that you would be obliged to stop until it cleared away, and in so doing you might perish with cold and wet. The alternative would be almost a certainty of falling headlong down one of these immense precipices, which I have mentioned before, 1,200 to 1,500 feet deep.

On Wednesday morning, about the same time, we made another attempt, and succeeded. The day was dry and clear, but there was a haze about the horizon which prevented us from seeing so far as we otherwise could have done. However, I suppose we had a clear view all round of not less than fifty miles; but no sail blessed our longing eyes. . . .

The Giant's Tomb is about 1,800 feet high, and the highest part of the land is on the south island, and is about 2,000 feet high. I also find that some of the chasms in the north-east angle of the land penetrate nearly (perhaps some of them go entirely) through the island, and are very narrow, with the mountains rising perpendicularly from the water to the height of 1,200 feet. Indeed some of them are so narrow that it appears as if a person could jump across at the top.

Sunday, October 16, 1864 . . . It is a surprising fact that the nearer to the water a seal is killed, the more tenacious it is of life. I have actually seen one of these black bull seals, with two bullets in him, his head split open with an axe, and his brains hanging out, dragging the men along the beach, who were trying to keep him out of the water by hanging on to his hind flappers; and he would have got away had not another man at that moment come to their assistance, and chopped off his head entirely with the ax.

But when they are at a great distance from the water a slight tap on the nose will stun them, and if struck immediately they will probably die without the slightest muscular motion. But in striking these fellows it is necessary to make sure of your blow, for if you miss they will have hold of you, and they would undoubtedly break the limb they got hold of. None of us as yet have got bit, thank God; but they have on one or two occasions taken the club out of some of our hands.

After getting our seal into the boat, we went as far as the

western head or entrance, where we got another black seal, and saw there three others, which we could have killed, but the two we had already got were a load for the boat. We also saw about half a dozen in the water, all black seals. Not very long ago we thought it would be impossible to eat this kind of seal; and indeed they are not by any means fit for food, for the strong smell of the meat is enough not only to disgust but to stifle a person. But what are starving men to do? and we may consider ourselves such. Hunger is certainly a good sauce. We were all in a state of excitement over the seal that was shot, for fear we should lose him and not be able to get any more.

Sunday, October 30, 1864. Here we are yet, closely clasped in Sarah's Bosom. I don't think I shall have any reason to dread purgatory after this; I trust that my purgations are now being performed, and are almost completed, for things appear to be drawing rapidly toward a crisis. The proverb says, when things are at their worst they must mend; but how bad that worst may be is beyond the reach of human knowledge.

I must now forego about the last bit of comfort that was left me, which is writing a little on Sundays; for if I continue to do so, my only remaining book of blank paper will be filled up. I may yet have something of moment to insert, for which purpose I must reserve the few remaining pages. So, my dear old book, I must bid you good bye, for God only knows how long. If nothing comes after us, we shall commence at the New Year to pull the *Grafton* to pieces and try what we can do with her bones. It is an undertaking the success of which I am exceedingly doubtful of.

Sunday, January 1, 1865. A whole year has now passed since I first anchored in this place, and in all probability another will at least pass before I get away, unless by chance of some sealers coming in the meantime.

I have got quite grey-headed. My hair is now all coming

out. Whether I shall get it again or remain baldheaded remains to be seen. I have also, since I last wrote, been very much troubled with boils, a number of which have been about my face; but these are going away again.

The men continue quite healthy, which is well, for I have not even a dose of salts to give them or take myself, whatever happens. The only medicine we have is plenty of exercise, which is not only conducive to health, but dispels gloom, and makes people really cheerful. I take plenty of this medicine myself, and encourage it in others as much as I possibly can; and I am happy to say the result has proven so far satisfactory.

I manage to keep the men almost constantly employed at something which is at the same time useful and amusing.

As the months went by, their clothes began to give out until they were in rags. Joseph's coat, the captain declared, would hardly have been a "circumstance" in comparison with some of theirs. Old canvas, old gunny-bags, and anything they got hold of, were used as patches, while canvas ravelings took the place of thread. All the sewing was done with a sail needle.

In the course of time they learned how to make sealskin leather. Even garments of the same material were attempted and completed, although it meant hours of painstaking effort.

In February, 1865, after thirteen months of captivity, the castaways determined to build a cutter of about ten tons, in which to make their way across the stormy seas to New Zealand. They stripped the wreck, taking all the iron ballast and available wood out of her. They found a block of iron among the ballast, which served their ingenious French mate as an anvil. They discovered on old saw file, but the teeth were all rusted off. Not at all discouraged, the Frenchman went to work. We read Musgrave's comments:

⚓

Sunday, February 5, 1865. Since I last wrote we have had some very severe weather. We had a rotatory gale, which continued without cessation from the 10th to the 25th of last month, during which time we were reduced to the point of starvation. It was impossible to launch the boat, and, although we traversed the shores as far as we could every day, we were unable to procure anything to eat. It rained heavily nearly all the time during the gale.

We have commenced in earnest the work of building a vessel to get away in. This will not prevent me from observing the Sabbath, but during the time mentioned it has been impossible to do so. Two Sundays we were out after grub; the next we were thatching the house; and last Sunday we were working at the wreck, trying to get her higher on the beach, to do which, with the means at my command, I have exhausted my ingenuity without success.

We stripped the lower masts and bowsprit, and cut them away; took every ounce of ballast out, and disburthened her of all possible weight, without taking away any of her upper work, as I did not know what I might have done with her had I succeeded in moving her. But this can only be done by lifting her bodily up. I had seventeen empty casks secured round her bows, but they had not the slightest impression on her. She is built of very heavy hard wood, principally greenheart and coppy. She was built from the wreck of a Spanish man-of-war; but I am sorry to say they took care not to put any copper bolts in her: but perhaps there were none in the original wreck.

But they have not been at all sparing with the iron. She has got any quantity of that about her, which will be of more service to me than any other part of her, excepting the plank, which is already full of bolt-holes; but we must make it answer our purpose. The vessel I am going to build will be a cutter of about ten tons. We have got the blocks laid down, and a quantity of timbers cut. All the frame shall have to get out of the woods, excepting the keel, which the *Grafton's* mainmast will supply.

⚓

Even after months of work under the able supervision of Mr. Raynal, who had natural talents as a builder, it was found that because of lack of proper tools the ship could never be finished. Up to this time the men had kept working in confident fashion, aiming for the eventual day when the craft would enter the water. Captain Musgrave, realizing that all was not well, had steeled himself for possible failure of the project. After the keel, stern, and sternpost had been constructed, both the captain and Raynal saw great trouble ahead. Finally the day came when the two men acknowledged to each other that forward progress had stopped forever. Mr. Raynal admitted without reservation that their limited tools prevented further construction.

The men had to be notified. The captain agreed that Mr. Raynal was the man to do it. On Sunday, March 12, Mr. Raynal called the others to him and gave them the stunning news that the vessel simply could not be completed.

In his journal for that day, the captain says of the incident:

⚓

It was truly deplorable to view the faces of all as we stood around him when he decidely pronounced it was impossible for him to make one. They all appeared, and I believe, no doubt felt, as if all hope were gone. It went like a shot to my heart, although I had begun to anticipate such a result and had made up my mind for action accordingly, but when I saw I must positively, as a last card, put my project into practice, I felt I was tempting Providence; for my tacit project and unalterable resolution, is to attempt a passage to Stewart's Island in the boat.

⟵

For months and months Captain Musgrave had pondered over this project of using the small boat, and finally his resolution was seconded by his crew. All but the cook were willing to risk the trip, and as he did not wish to stay behind, he also then gave in. Of course, the boat was "old and shaky," but Musgrave was determined to strengthen her, to lengthen her about three feet and to raise her sides about twelve inches. They all went to work in high spirits to fit their boat for sea.

On March 26 the captain entered in his diary this passage:

⚓

The sea booms and the wind howls. These are sounds which have been almost constantly ringing in my ears for the last fifteen months; for, during the whole of that time, I venture to say that they have not been hushed more than a fortnight together.

⟵

Six days a week, from daylight till half-past nine at night they worked at the boat under the direction of Mr. Raynal, who had unusual boatbuilding ability. One day the gimlet broke! They were in dread that the accident would stop the work, but they were able to repair it.

Their greatest enemies were the flies. The captain remembered other places where the mosquitoes were bothersome, but nowhere were they so malignant as these flies. At Auckland the sandflies swarmed by the million, covering every part of the skin that happened to be exposed, and even were able to work inside the clothing, biting fiercely. The captain stated that he could not find an area the size of a pin where the flies had not blistered him.

A terrific hurricane postponed the departure from the island, but at last they were ready for sea. Two men backed out, preferring to stay and risk starvation rather than brave the present perils of the stormy seas in the small boat. They were left behind. The captain, mate, and one sailor set sail northward for Stewart's Island, just south of New Zealand.

Twenty miles out they were overtaken by the full fury of a southwest gale. The boat began to leak, but they kept the pump going nearly all the time. The fierce seas broke incessantly over the little craft until it was a wonder that she stayed together. But she did. With the determination and perseverance of the captain and crew, the small boat landed them five days later at Port Adventure on Stewart's Island.

The captain wrote:

I had not eaten an ounce of food from the time of leaving until we arrived, and only drank about half a pint of water; yet I felt no fatigue until the night before we landed, when I suddenly became quite exhausted, and lay down on the deck, over which there was water washing, for the first time since we left the island. We were now close to the land. I lay for about half an hour, and then got up again, feeling that I had sufficient strength to enable me to hold out till the next day; but had we been out any longer, I feel convinced that I should never have put my foot on shore again.

ᚷ

As the captain had promised to rescue his two companions left at Auckland Isles, he began at once to interest the citizens of Port Adventure in the project. Money was raised and a vessel fitted out, with Captain Musgrave as pilot and guide and a Stewart Islander named Captain Cross as master. The passage back was only a little less perilous than the trip to Stewart's Island. Again and again they were in imminent danger of being wrecked.

They finally sailed north of the island and found traces of another crew that had been wrecked on the hidden reefs there. Whether it was the camp for the *Invercauld* survivors will never be known. Musgrave and his men searched the shores and adjacent woods, and at last found, half-buried beneath the fallen roof of a rude hut, the body of a sailor who had evidently perished from hunger. A slate lay near him. It had been written on, but one word only could be deciphered—JAMES. He was buried by the captain and his companions.

"This melancholy incident," wrote Captain Musgrave, "would undoubtedly give rise to serious thoughts in any one, but how infinitely more in me, whose bones might, at the present moment, have been lying above the ground under similar circumstances, had not the hand of Providence showered such great mercies upon me, perhaps the least deserving."

Captain Musgrave did find his companions. Let his own words tell how:

⚓

It was very showery in the forenoon, but at noon the showers took off, and at three P.M. the wind moderated a little, and we at once got under weigh, and, under double reefed

canvas, beat up to our old house; and as we did not come up
in sight of it until within about a mile from it, the boys did
not see us until we were close upon them. Then the one who
saw us ran into the house to tell the other, and before they
reached the beach Captain Cross and myself had landed, leaving the cutter under weigh, as there was too much wind and
sea to anchor her. One of them, the cook, on seeing me, turned
as pale as a ghost, and staggered up to a post, against which he
leaned for support, for he was evidently on the point of faint-
ing, while the other, George, seized my hand in both of his,
and gave my arm a severe shaking, crying, "Captain Musgrave,
how are ye?" apparently unable to say anything else.

The castaways did ample justice to their first civilized dinner. They told the captain that they had been very much
pinched for food since he had left them and that on one occasion they were obliged to catch mice and eat them. They also
did not agree very well, and were actually on the point of
separating and living apart.

The return trip was far from a pleasure cruise. Here is one
representative entry in the captain's logbook:

September 7. Hard gale and high, dangerous sea. The
little vessel is being knocked about unmercifully. Heavy rain.
No place to lie down. Blankets and every stitch of clothing
wringing wet. Can't cook anything, even a cup of tea. Second
edition of our trip in the boat. Misery. Four P.M.: Blowing
a hurricane; sea frightful; vessel laboring and straining
immensely; if not very strong she cannot stand this long; consider her in a highly dangerous condition. Just taken in

mainsail and jib, and set a small boat's sail, under which she feels somewhat easier; but if one of the high seas coming round her in every direction falls on board, she is gone; it would knock her in ten thousand pieces. Frightful. Midnight, at six P.M.: The gale began to moderate, and fortunately the sea quickly followed suit. We set the mainsail, but carried away the traveler and tore the sail. Eight P.M.: The wind came from the S.W. and continues very light, but sufficient to keep her steady, while the sea is rapidly running down, hope soon to be able to make her stretch her legs again. She has weathered this storm bravely, and without sustaining any visible damage about the hull. Surprising what these little vessels will stand; but she is an amazingly good sea-boat, rides like a sea-gull, and holds her ground well. Bravo, *Flying Scud*.

They all landed safely. When the inhabitants learned of the situation, they were anxious to raise a fund for the shipwrecked mariners in order to clothe and shelter them. Within a short time enough money was made available so that the more pressing wants of the sailors were satisfied.

Honest Captain Musgrave requested nothing more, however, than that his draft on his owners might be cashed.

"And thus," wrote the admirable captain, "with a grateful heart I end my journal; with what deep thankfulness to a gracious Providence for saving myself and my companions from a miserable fate I trust I need not here set down."

I have already mentioned that the crews from two shipwrecked craft were on the island together for a year without either group discovering the other.

Details of the *Invercauld* shipwreck disaster, when compared to the fine journal which Captain Musgrave wrote, are at best fragmentary. The ship *Invercauld,* a vessel of 888 tons, became a total wreck on the northwest end of the Auckland Islands on the night of May 10, 1864. Six sailors drowned and nineteen others got ashore safely. There was nothing saved from the wreck at first, but later they went back to the scene and found two pounds of biscuits and three pounds of pork.

With the aid of matches which had been rescued from the ship, they made a fire. Remaining at the site of the wreck for four days, those who could do so climbed to the top of the island, which was about two thousand feet high, the upper reaches being almost perpendicular. The only food they found the first few days were roots of wild shrubs, but they did discover plenty of fresh water. As it was the start of the winter, it grew very cold, and the men worked hard to erect a shelter from tree boughs, after which they huddled around a fire.

The next morning they started for a bay on the east side but, as there was no path, did not get there for several days. Four men died during this interval.

Reaching the bay, they found and ate some limpets which were on the rocks, and then managed to catch two seals, finding them very good food.

The days became weeks, and then months, and the diet of limpets, roots, and water was not enough to sustain life. By the end of August every man was dead except three—Captain George Dalgarno, his mate, Andrew Smith, and a seaman named Robert Holding. They managed to live, however, for twelve months and ten days, finally being picked up by the Portuguese ship *Julian* sailing for Callao with Chinese passengers. The only reason the *Julian* stopped was that she was leaking badly and had sent a boat on shore for material with which to repair the ship.

They found the three survivors who were taken to Callao, Peru, reaching there June 28, 1865. Without question the survivors from the *Grafton* and *Invercauld* were on the island at the same time, but the smoke which Captain Musgrave saw in the distance one day could not have been the campfire of the castaways belonging to the *Invercauld,* for they had already left the island by then. The dead body and the slate containing some obliterated writing, also discovered by Captain Musgrave, may have belonged to this party, but we shall never know.

The Aucklands were discovered by Captain Abraham Bristow, in the ship *Ocean,* a vessel belonging to the late Samuel Enderby, Esq., during a whaling voyage, August 16, 1806. The following extract from his logbook, quoted by Sir James Ross, announces the discovery: ". . . at daylight saw land. This island or islands, as being the first discoverer, I shall call *Lord Auckland's* (my friend through my father)."

Captain Morrell, an American navigator, visited the Auckland Isles in 1829. In the year 1840 the island was visited by the vessels of three nations—the English ships *Erebus* and *Terror,* under Sir James Clark Ross and Captain Crozier; the French corvettes *L'Astrolabe* and *La Zelee,* under Dumont D'Urville; and the United States Exploring Expedition, under Captain Charles Wilkes.

The "Great Southern Whale Fishery" was established here in 1850, but in less than two years the whole scheme fell through.

Captain Morrell tells us that the formation of the Auckland Islands is volcanic and that they are constituted chiefly of basalt and greenstone. Deas Head, in Laurie Harbour north of Shoe Island, is of great geological interest, exhibiting fine columns three hundred feet high, which are highly magnetic. The loftiest hill, Mount Eden, at the head of Laurie Harbour, attains an elevation of 1,325 feet, is rounded at the top, and is clothed with grass to its summit. Another hill in the west rises to nearly a thousand feet. Near a watering place a commodious hut had been erected by a French whaler. Nearby there was another in ruins, and close to it the grave of a French sailor, whose name was inscribed on a wooden cross erected over it.

Although the Auckland Islands are considered spectacular in their beauty, for the two crews of sailors who were battered ashore there in the year 1864 it was an island of unhappiness, sorrow, and death.

12

THE ST. GEORGE'S BAY HORROR

On a cold wintry day in the year 1868 an anxious wife left her home at St. George's, Newfoundland, to go down to the shore. As her husband's ship was long overdue, she was worried about his safety. When the water came in sight, she was amazed to see drifting islands of ice extending to the horizon, which she realized were probably to blame for the delay in her husband's arrival.

The housewife began to walk along the beach, every so often stopping to glance far out over the ice. The only signs of life she noticed were sea gulls, wild ducks, and an occasional smaller bird. Reaching the end of her walk, which was made with the wind at her back, she turned, buttoned her coat at the neck, and started toward home.

Moments later she glanced seaward once more. To her amazement far in the distance was a tiny black form. She simply couldn't believe it! She kept staring, and as she did so, the black form seemed to move. Hurrying back to her residence, she ran into the old-fashioned parlor to pick up a pair of opera glasses which her mother had brought from Paris years ago. Although they were of a relatively small power, they might possibly help her to make out what the object was. She sped with the opera glasses to the beach. Leaning against one of the pilings on the fishermen's wharf there, she fastened her gaze on the distant horizon. To her amazement there were now two figures.

So excited was she by this time that she hastened to the home of a neighbor and asked him to get down a venerable telescope which he owned and go with her to the beach.

Fifteen minutes later he was staring out at the same part of the horizon.

"Well," she said, "what do you see?"

"Believe it or not, I see three black forms out there! No, now I see four!"

In this strange manner the people of Newfoundland learned of one of the most astounding maritime tragedies in the entire history of that island.

Accounts of piratical cruelty at sea have often amazed me, but the tale of the seven stowaways from the merchant ship *Arran* off the shores of Newfoundland has impressed me with an overwhelming realization of how thoughtlessly brutal man can be to man.

George Blake, in his *Down to the Sea,* tells us that the deeds of Captain Robert Watt and Mate James Kerr in their fiendish treatment of the stowaways represent "a record of cruelty and suffering on an almost heroic scale." Many men have called the unbelievable story of what occurred on the wooden sailing ship and later on the ice one of the most ghastly on record.

On April 7, 1868, the 1,063-ton *Arran* sailed from Greenock, Scotland, bound for the New World with a cargo of oakum and coal. The master was Robert Watt, a native of Saltcoats in Ayrshire. The mate, James Kerr, was the captain's brother-in-law and came from the Isle of Arran. There were twenty-four others in the ship's company.

The usual inspection for stowaways revealed the presence of two boys, who were promptly put ashore. The *Arran* continued sailing out to sea. As the ship was leaving the Irish Channel the carpenter began to batten down the hatches for the long voyage to America. Then, as if on cue, no less than seven other stowaways emerged one by one from various hiding places around the ship. All boys and young men, they were David Brand, 16; James Bryson, 16; Peter Currie, 12; Hugh M'Ginnes, 11; John Paul, 11; Hugh M'Ewan, 11 and 22-year-old Bernard Reilly. We probably will never know the details of why these young people hid aboard the *Arran*. Possibly they wanted to go to America in search of work, but if this were so, it was not brought out in any fashion at the trial later. Perhaps the youths, who came from vastly different social and economic backgrounds, had no conception of the long distance to America.

By the time the boys were discovered, Captain Watt decided that it was far too late for the *Arran* to turn back to Scotland. If he had known what lay ahead, however, he might have returned to Greenock at all costs and put the youngsters back ashore.

Although willing to work at first, the boys soon became seasick and were sent below. Nor were they dressed for the activities of a sailor at sea in the wintry season. Later, in a letter back to Scotland a crew member gave a graphic description of the terrible conditions to which the stowaways were subjected:

The boys were thinly clad, and were not able to stand the severe cold. The men could hardly stand it, let alone the boys. Two of the little ones had their feet bare, and as we were going too far to the northward amongst hail, frost, snow and raining continually, none of them would keep on deck to work. As soon as the mate missed them, he went with a rope's end in hand and ordered them out, and as they came out gave them a walloping, and pretty often very severely. The captain never interfered with the mate's handling of the situation until one good day when the hatches were all opened. On going to shift some oakum and coils of rope where the stowaways slept, the crew found the boys all besmeared with filth. Then Captain Watt gave them a thrashing, and made all hands clean it up.

⚓

For some reason, the mate was especially anxious to do everything he could to make the life of young James Bryson miserable, and he succeeded. Continually flogged and starved, the lad had a terrible existence.

Finally on May 10, 1868, while in Cabot Straits between Cape Breton and Newfoundland, the *Arran* ran into a terrible pack of floating ice. Soon she was hopelessly trapped by the floe and carried into St. George's Bay, Newfoundland.

The captain and mate decided that they were "fed up" with the stowaways and agreed to take steps to get rid of the boys. Giving them only a biscuit apiece, the officers ordered six of them to go down on the ice and make their way to shore. The mate, a friend of twelve-year-old Peter Currie's father, allowed Peter to stay on board.

Actually the naked eye revealed no land in sight, but the captain later claimed that at the time he could see a settlement with his high-powered telescope. "There were houses and people dwelling in them not so far away," Captain Watt asserted. In addition there was a craft, the *Myrtle*, embedded in the ice two and one-half miles distant.

Probably when the boys were put over the side onto the ice they were no closer than fourteen miles from land. It is hard to picture what the boys faced when they were forced down from the ship in freezing weather. They were starving, barefooted, and dressed in ragged clothes. It is a wonder that any of them survived to tell their story later.

When the letter from the crewman arrived in Greenock, telling of the abandoning of the stowaways, the relatives of the missing boys soon found out what really had happened. At first they were horrified and then they were furious. Within a few days the whole community was talking about nothing but the boys on the ice. Weeks went by. Then, on the evening of July 30, 1868, the *Arran* came up the Clyde. Several hours later she approached her pier.

By this time a hostile crowd was awaiting her arrival. The moment she was warped close enough to the pier, several determined men jumped aboard and started looking for the captain and his mate. Forewarned by the crew, Watt and Kerr locked themselves in the cabin. The police soon arrived on the scene and put a guard aboard the vessel to prevent violence. The crowd, however, remained until eleven o'clock that night.

On the morning of the next day the captain and the mate were taken before the local sheriff where they were formally charged. Their alleged crime was "cruelly and maliciously compelling one or more of Her Majesty's lieges to leave a ship while said ship was embedded in ice at a considerable distance from land, to the imminent risk and serious and permanent injury to their persons."

At that time it was not known to the authorities that two of the boys had lost their lives as a result of the inhuman actions of the captain and mate. Nevertheless, bail was refused and both Captain Watt and Mate Kerr were committed for trial. Meanwhile the Purcurator-Fiscal had telegraphed across the ocean to Newfoundland. The reply from America contained the stunning information that two of the boys had perished on the ice, while four had reached shore. Three of them were still at St. George's Bay.* Little Hugh M'Ewan and Hugh M'Ginnes, both eleven, had never reached land!

The charge against the two prisoners now became culpable homicide. Later, however, for reasons never satisfactorily explained, this count was dropped and changed to "assault, cruel and barbarous usage, and the innominate offense of compelling the boys to leave the ship to the danger of their lives."

Meanwhile, across the ocean the surviving boys were taken in a schooner to St. Johns, where they embarked on the brigantine *Hannah and Bennie*. They reached Greenock safely on October 1, 1868, not quite six months after they had stowed away on the *Arran*.

With the boys back in Scotland, the authorities decided that the trial should begin. The proceedings occupied the twenty-third, twenty-fourth, and twenty-fifth of November, 1868.

The first of the young witnesses was James Bryson, who explained how he and his companions had climbed aboard the *Arran*, hiding in the hold for the night. After the ship sailed, they remained out of sight all the next day and part of the night, being without food or water all that time.

James was hiding in the hold when he noticed the carpenter battening down the hatches. Just before it was too late, his friend Brand knocked against the bottom of the hatchway, thus allowing the carpenter to discover them. Bryson and his friend were seasick for the next four days, during which time Bryson had been scrubbed and flogged with the lead line.

* Bernard Reilly, the eldest, had gone to seek work at Halifax, Nova Scotia.

"The mate flogged me when I was sitting on one of the hatches," testified Bryson. "I was made to take off my jacket, waistcoat and shirt, leaving only my semmit (undershirt) on. The coil was about one half inch thick. The mate flogged me for about three minutes. The blows were very painful. I cried out because of the pain I was suffering. When I was screaming, the master of the vessel came forward. The mate made me strip off the rest of my clothing. I was then made to lie down on the deck."

Both the master and the mate were present, according to Bryson. Robert Hunter, one of the crew, was ordered to draw salt water in a bucket and throw it on Bryson, although the weather was very cold.

"The captain then scrubbed me with a hair broom all over my body," continued Bryson, "giving me great pain. The mate then took the broom up and scrubbed me harder than the captain.

"I made many attempts to rise during the scrubbing. When the captain was scrubbing, the mate was standing over me with a rope in his hand, with which he threatened to strike me if I attempted to run away. After the mate had scrubbed me, he handed the broom to Brand and told him to scrub me with it.

"I felt pain during the scrubbing, but not afterwards. After the scrubbing was finished I was made to wash my clothes. I was ordered to the forecastle by the mate. I was naked at the time. When I had been there about an hour my coat and semmit were returned. I suffered very much from exposure. My body had not dried."

The court was now told how the captain and the mate climbed over the side to walk across the ice. After they had gone, the boys began looking for food. Finding some biscuits, they filled their pockets. Then Bryson found some currants in a keg, but could discover nothing else.

"I was hungry," Bryson said. "I took about a fistful of currants and returned to my work of scraping the deck. The mate was coming up the vessel's side when he saw me coming out of the cabin. He ordered my hands to be tied, and Brand and I were searched. The mate gave the order. Nothing was found on Brand.

"My pocket was cut on the outside and the currants 'kepped' in a saucer. The captain ordered the currants to be given to the other boys. I was afterwards stripped naked by order of the mate. The captain was present all the time and saw what took place. The mate placed my head on the deck, seized my legs, and held them up to his breast while the captain flogged me. He gave me fifteen to twenty lashes.

"The ship at this time was surrounded by ice, but was not frozen in. I was ordered by the mate to help the boy Currie to scrub the deck when I was stark naked. I was so engaged for about ten minutes. After sweeping the deck, the mate sent me to the house in the forecastle, where I remained for about a quarter of an hour, when I was called out and my semmit was returned to me. I was then placed on the hatch, and the mate told me to tell him all that I had done in my life."

David Brand, sixteen, stated that he was present when Bryson was flogged. The temperature was probably just a little above freezing. Brand testified that as Bryson was dirty, Brand was given orders to scrub him to get the dirt off. It was a hard broom that Brand was given to scrub Bryson, and it took about ten minutes.

Brand explained that the mate flogged Bryson for two minutes after he had been scrubbed. "There were about thirty blows given during that time. I saw marks on his person after the flogging was over. The captain was present during the flogging, but said or did nothing. I saw blood on Bryson's back after the flogging was over. He remained naked after the flogging.

"I stole some biscuits and a piece of beef out of the cabin to eat. Bryson went in afterwards and took some currants. He was seen by the mate, who ordered him to be searched. The captain afterwards flogged him for about two or three minutes. . . .

"The captain said he would make them go on the ice presently. Hugh M'Ginnes asked the captain what he would do on the ice with his bare feet. The captain replied that it would be as well for him to die on the ice as in the ship, as he would get no more food there.

"Paul was crying bitterly. He cried out, 'Oh, my fingers!' I do not know why he cried that out. Paul was the last one that went on the ice. None of us got any breakfast that morning. We went away from the ship without tasting any food. Biscuits were thrown overboard after we left the ship—one biscuit to each."

When eleven-year-old John Paul took the stand, he explained in his testimony how he had become a stowaway, hiding in the forecastle head. He had not come out until the tug towing her away from land had left the *Arran*.

"I was poorly clad when I went on board. I had no shoes on and had no clothes except those I was wearing. I took no clothes or provisions with me. There were other stowaways on board. M'Ginnes was clad the same as myself. No shoes were supplied to me on board. I got canvas to make trousers, but it was taken from me again some days after, before I left the ship. It was taken back because I could not get them made.

"I remember Bryson being scrubbed some days before we left the ship. He was scrubbed with a 'kyar' broom—a hard broom with which they swept the decks.

"When we were going to be put on the ice I hid myself. I was brought forward, and asked the mate to keep me on board. He said he would have nothing to do with it. When on the rails I was struck by the captain with a belaying pin, because I would not go on the ice. I was the last to leave the ship."

When Brand refused to go over the side the captain grabbed him by the collar and forced him over. The eleven-year-old Paul now fled to the forecastle, but the captain found him and brought him out.

Reilly was the first to go down on the ice and the others followed. Peter Currie, the stowaway who was allowed to remain on board, later testified that he heard the mate say he would wager any man on board twenty pounds sterling that the boys would be back to their dinner on the ship.

The condition of the boys was almost beyond belief. Both Paul and M'Ginnes had bare feet. M'Ewan had boots and was better clothed than the others. They left the ship just before nine o'clock in the morning in clear daylight.

Not one man in the crew protested in any way when the boys were put overboard onto the floating ice, but afterwards they admitted in court that they "thought it too dangerous to put the boys off." The excuse for their silence was that they did not dare interfere with the captain or they could have been charged with mutiny.

Bryson said that the boys had no idea how far the land was. "We saw a black haze, but nothing else. I thought we might as well die on the ice as on board the vessel. We were twelve hours on the ice that day. We found the journey very dangerous. We had gone about ten or eleven miles before we met with danger; it was near the shore. The ice had been pretty good, but there it was all broken. I fell into the water up to the neck while jumping from one piece of ice to another.

"We all fell into crevices at various times. We got out the best way we could, each had just to scramble for himself. M'Ewan fell in once and I pulled him out; he fell in a second time and scrambled out himself; the third time he went down and never came up, the ice closed over him. It was hopeless to attempt to save him. . . .

"Some hours after this happened M'Ginnes sat down on a piece of ice and said he could go no farther. We urged him to come along with us, and said if he did not, he knew what would become of him. . . . No attempt was made to assist him; we had enough to do to assist ourselves, going all day across the ice barefooted. . . . We heard his cries a long way behind us, although we could not see him."

Late that day they reached the end of the ice field. By this time they could see land and houses, but there was a very substantial area of open water between them and the shore. Bryson, Reilly, and Brand decided to make a desperate attempt to reach shore by using ice cakes which had broken from the floe. Arming themselves with fragments of wood, they began paddling toward the distant land. A short time later they were sighted by the woman walking along the beach who called for help. Rescuers quickly launched a boat and within a short time plucked the boys off the ice cakes just as the sun was sinking. The last boy taken from the floe was John Paul.

Additional testimony was now heard concerning the two lost boys.

"When M'Ewan fell in the third time," said Bryson, "it was about midday. The others were about a hundred yards ahead of me at that time; I then ran on. I do not know why none of the rest looked round any more than I did. I looked no more after M'Ewan. M'Ginnes sat down, tired, about five miles from the shore. I never stopped; I left him sitting.

"I heard him for about a hundred yards off, I dare say—for about ten minutes; the ice was bad, and we could not go extra fast at that time." They told the people on shore that M'Ewan and M'Ginnes had been left behind. Nothing more was heard of them while the boys remained at St. George's Bay.

The members of the crew attempted to minimize the

cruelty with which the stowaways were treated throughout the voyage; but none could deny the brutalities to which Bryson was subjected, nor the fact that the boys were forced to leave the ship.

The testimony of crewman George Henry was particularly important in explaining why the crew did not interfere and stop the barbaric activities.

"Three of the little boys were unwilling to go," said Henry. "They began to cry when they were asked to go by the mate, and continued to do so when they went away."

A juryman then spoke to Seaman Henry.

"Why did you not interfere when you thought the boys were going to be placed in such danger?"

"I had no right to interfere with my master and mate; I was a servant."

"If the master or mate had been going to murder the boys, would you have interfered?"

"There was a chance of their reaching shore, and some of them did reach it."

The captain declared that he had "invited" the boys to leave the ship and have a run on the ice. "I pointed out to them houses on the shore, and said to them they might have a fine run ashore!" He admitted that he had made no inquiries on shore as to their fate, and did not know what had become of them.

The mate stated that he never caused Bryson to be scrubbed with a hard brush, neither did he ever assault him or strike him with a rope. He claimed he did not force or compel the boys to leave the ship. He never attempted to find out what became of them, however.

Eventually, James Kerr pleaded guilty of assault, and the Solicitor-General accepted the plea and withdrew the charge of culpable homicide in the case of the mate.

From the evidence there could be little doubt that the boys

had been compelled to leave the ship. They did not voluntarily quit the vessel on so perilous a journey as that which they had to take.

The whole of the evidence pointed clearly to the fact that the boy who sank in the water, the one who was left to perish upon the ice, and the survivors who were more or less injured by the exposure and fatigue they were compelled to undergo owed their deaths and injuries to the criminal act of the master of the *Arran*, by whose orders they were made to leave the ship. The master had, without question, been guilty of the crime of "culpable homicide."

Defense attorney Young surprised everyone by stating that it would surprise no one if both M'Ewan and M'Ginnes were to turn up alive and well. Of course, he was wrong.

After going over the evidence, the Lord Justice-Clerk announced that it proved force was exercised by the captain toward the boys to make them leave the vessel. His Lordship commented on the indifference shown by the captain as to the fate of the boys.

After reviewing the evidence as to the flogging and scrubbing of the lad Bryson, his Lordship said that, if the jury believed that death had been occasioned by the captain's authority or instrumentality, they would come to the conclusion as to his guilt.

His Lordship concluded by saying that the case was a very important one—the first of the kind that had ever come before the tribunals of that court.

The jury retired at twenty minutes to three o'clock that November afternoon in 1868. After an absence of thirty-five minutes the members returned to the court with the following verdict:

"On the two charges of assault the jury are unanimously of the opinion that the captain is not guilty; that he is guilty of the charge of culpable homicide; that he is guilty of compelling the boys to leave a British ship; but that, on account of his previous good character, they recommend him to the leniency of the court."

The jury found the mate guilty of assault, according to his own confession.

The Dean of Faculty then addressed the court in mitigation of the sentence of the mate, arguing it was impossible to maintain discipline on board a ship unless there was the power of chastisement in the hands of the superior officer.

Mr. Charles Scott said that he had intended to address the court in behalf of his client (the captain), but after the recommendation of the jury he would not do so.

The Lord Justice-Clerk then sentenced the mate to four months' imprisonment and the captain to eighteen months' imprisonment.

The result was received by the audience with loud hisses of indignation at the "astounding lightness of the sentences."

Captain Watt was then twenty-eight. Of average height he wore an attractive beard and moustache much lighter than his dark brown hair.

Mate James Kerr, however, was of tougher fiber. A rough, thin creature with a dark beard, he was coarse and domineering. Yet he was kind to Currie, whose people he knew well, even arranging for the lad's passage back to Scotland.

It is probable that the stowaways of the *Arran* would have come to no great harm if Captain Watt alone had been in control of their treatment. The habits of some of the children were dirty, and there was some theft, though under provocation, and the situation found James Kerr quite willing to resort to harsh measures.

Many of the physical brutalities which the mate showed toward the boys might have had some excuse, but there is no question that he was unnecessarily cruel on several occasions.

Indeed the officers of the *Arran,* regardless of how the lads bothered them, should be condemned for their sadistic treatment. But there are scores and scores of instances of similar cases at sea occurring during the nineteenth century, while even worse are the cases in earlier times of known cruelty of men to their fellow humans out of sight of land.

Writers often blame the sea itself for the brutality which occurred aboard ships, but some of the human torturers who sailed their vessels a century and more ago carried out fiendish and inhuman acts for which the sea could not possibly be blamed. The *Arran* story is a case in point.

13

AN UNUSUAL INCIDENT

Every one of the seven seas has sometime been the scene of a seeming miracle. One that has particularly interested me concerns a Captain Samuel Wroughton of Newburyport, Massachusetts, who, during a period of depression in American shipping activity in 1876, took command of the British schooner *Caribbean,* sailing her to Aspinwall, Panama, the port now identified as Colon.

When the *Caribbean* was tied up to a pier at Aspinwall, Captain Wroughton took a walk down the main street from Howard House toward the office of the British consul at the railroad depot. Stepping up onto the sidewalk, a man suddenly confronted the captain. Respectfully he tipped his hat in a sailorlike manner and introduced himself as Abraham Sherrie.

"I understand, sir, that you are the captain of the schooner *Caribbean?*"

"I am, but what is that to you?"

"I am on the beach here, sir, and wish to work my passage to Jamaica, which I have discovered is your next stop. I have had a lot of trouble because I got drunk and was thrown into jail. It was a long time since I had been ashore, and I guess I drank a little too much and enjoyed the company of too many girls here for too long a period. But I am ready to go to sea again, sir. All I want to do is to work my way to Jamaica."

The captain sized him up. The out-of-work sailor was a man of less than middle height, but strongly built. His arms were longer than average length for his size. His head was disproportionately large and carried a shaggy growth of black hair.

Short a man in his crew, Captain Wroughton agreed to meet Sherrie the following morning at the office of the British consul, as the *Caribbean* sailed under the flag of England. Although not necessarily believing all Sherrie told him, Wroughton decided to take the man aboard. There in the consul's office, the captain accepted the sailor as a work-a-way to Jamaica. The master of the schooner watched the man as he slowly, laboriously inscribed his name in a peculiar hand. Captain Wroughton decided there was something strange about this individual, but for the life of him he could not guess what it was. The sailor sensed that the master of the *Caribbean* was watching him sign his name with more than usual attention. He had signed the articles as Abraham Sherrie with his left hand. Sherrie explained that he had lost the thumb and first two fingers of his right hand when they were frozen during a whaling voyage in the Arctic Ocean in 1871. He told the details of the incident.

Five years before in the Arctic Circle he was out on the ice with a group of men killing seals that were desperately needed for meat. A sudden snowstorm soon became a howling hurricane, forcing Sherrie and other members of the party to be separated from the ship for more than seventy-two hours. By the time they were able to get back aboard his right hand was frozen severely. Later, after he returned to the ship, gangrene set in. The doctor tried desperately to save his hand but had been forced to amputate the thumb and two fingers.

When Sherrie learned to write again with his left hand, he

printed the initial of both his given name and surname instead of writing it as he did the remainder of the name.

Abrahams Sherrie

To protect his new crew member from the temptations of women and wine ashore, Captain Wroughton ordered his mate to take the man aboard the schooner at once. Two days later, by the time the *Caribbean* sailed out of the harbor, Sherrie had become a decided favorite with the crew, in addition to which he proved himself an outstanding seaman. Although his face was clean-shaven, his appearance was unusual. Deep pits in his cheeks identified him as a smallpox victim, but the worst blemish was a jagged knife wound which had laid his left cheek open from the eyelid to the upper lip. In the process of healing, the wound had pulled the muscles of his face in a strange way, leaving the corner of his mouth drawn up a quarter of an inch higher on his left side than his right. This made Sherrie's face have the perpetual appearance of a weird and most unnatural grin. Although his chest was covered with a dense mat of hair, his limbs, as his face, were as hairless as a child's.

He claimed that he was a native of Newfoundland, but his strange English accent identified him unmistakably to another sailor as a native of England's Somersetshire. Sherrie could speak four languages fairly well: English, Spanish, German, and French. Although he swore fluently in other tongues, the crew noticed that he never uttered a profane word in English.

After leaving Aspinwall harbor, Captain Wroughton charted a course for Kingston, Jamaica, which would take him on a dead beat to windward from the lower Central American ports. Unfortunately, the schooner was caught in a terrific

storm and was blown far inshore. When the palm trees of Le
Fuerte Islands were sighted, some distance out to sea from
Cartagena Harbor, the captain became concerned for the
safety of his vessel. Fortunately the intense gale moderated the
next day and the *Caribbean* resumed her course.

Heavy squalls of rain had accompanied the gale, necessita-
ting the presence of the crew on deck all that night. In the
downpour, every man suffered severely from exposure, but
Abraham Sherrie was the only one seriously affected. Collapsing at dawn while furling a jib, he almost fell into the sea,
but the other sailors grabbed him and carried him below.
Seaman Sherrie ran a fever that day and could not report for
duty the following morning. Wroughton decided that Abraham's fever was due at least in part to his excesses while enjoying the wild night life at Aspinwall. Unfortunately as the day
wore on, Sherrie became noticeably worse.

Worried about the condition of his seaman, Captain
Wroughton set up a makeshift hospital bunk in his own cabin
and had the crew take turns watching the ailing mariner. Four
days passed without a sign of improvement. By this time the
schooner was approaching the dangerous Baxo Nuevo Reef,
weathering it April 1. That afternoon one of the men tending
the jib sheet looked down in the forecastle hatch.

"My God, Sherrie is in trouble," he shouted. The captain
was called and went down the ladder to the deck of the forecastle. There he found Sherrie lying on his face with one arm
doubled under his chest and the other wound around the bottom of the ladder. Assuming that Sherrie had tried to get up
from his bunk for some reason, the captain reached down to
help the man to his feet. Abraham Sherrie, however, was cold
in death. His limbs were rigid, and his usually florid skin had
faded to the dry texture of parchment. His eyes were like yellow balls. The pupils, having been rolled up under the eye-
lids, were quite hardened. The most terrible feature was

Sherrie's face, for the hand of death had fashioned an awful caricature of the sardonic expression which characterized it in life. Every distorted line of his physiognomy seemed to grin into space with a horrific, sightless leer. Apparently the body was already in *rigor mortis,* so it seemed that he must have died some hours before.

Captain Wroughton now had a decision to make. Should he sail for the nearest port and allow Sherrie to have a decent burial ashore, or should he order his sailors down into the hold to bring up some coral rock ballast and prepare the lifeless body for sea burial? He talked the matter over with his crew, none of whom was anxious to have the grinning sightless face of the luckless mariner remain aboard the *Caribbean* any longer than absolutely necessary. Yielding to their wishes, the captain announced that the funeral would take place at four bells that afternoon.

Wroughton had always had a horror of either being buried at sea, or having to go through the necessity of conducting a service for a sailor who died at sea. He now called his men together. "I'm in a tough situation," he explained. "I've never had to do this before. Reading about death at sea is vastly different from taking part in sea burial, but let's all do the best we can."

Within the hour Captain Wroughton had worked out a simple ceremony of which the men approved. The body with fifty pounds of coral rock attached to each ankle, was laid out on common pine plank. Promptly as four bells rang out from the ship's clock, the captain began reading slowly from the Bible. When the passage ended, Wroughton raised his hand, and two appointed seamen lifted the end of the plank. Because of their nervousness, the body caught in some peculiar way as it slid down the wooden board, so that the plank went with it into the sea. The horrified seamen watched the pine board and its burden as they sank beneath the waves.

The schooner now slowly gathered headway and resumed her course. Suddenly one of the seamen who had been awed but fascinated by the entire affair shouted to the others: "Sherrie has slipped his ballast and is coming to the surface!"

The others rushed to the schooner's taffrail, but by this time whatever the sailor had seen was too far astern to be identified. The *Caribbean,* now gaining way before a ten-knot quarter breeze, was soon hull down, far from the scene of the burial. All that remained of Abraham Sherrie aboard the schooner was a suitable entry of death and burial in the log and the recollection of them in the minds of his former messmates.

The weeks went by. The usual stops in the West Indies were made by the trader. April gave way to May, and the summer turned to fall.

On September 30, business called Captain Wroughton to the office of Robert Bentwick, the British consul at St. Thomas in the Virgin Islands. The *Caribbean* was safely tied up at a nearby pier.

As the consul was out of the room for the moment, Wroughton sat down at the official's desk to await his return. Resting on the table at the captain's elbow was a great heap of newspapers and documents. To pass the time the master picked up a newspaper, knocking two of the lighter papers to the floor. Leaning over to pick them up, he suddenly stiffened as he received a shock.

On one of the documents dated July 11, 1876, was the signature of the man whose dead body he had ordered dropped overboard far at sea earlier that year! The calligraphy was unmistakable. The name had been affixed to the printed form of a consular instrument noting the committal to the public hospital of a passenger from the bark *Soldene* out of Belize. The document was signed by the subject himself, Abraham Sherrie. The signature was written in the same curious angular character with which the article had been signed, with the backward inclination of the letters common to those who use their left hand. The initial letters of the given name and surname were in printed capitals!

Fascinated by this document, Captain Wroughton studied it closely. The date, July 11, 1876, was unmistakable. So was the signature of the man he had buried within sight of the white water of Baxo Nuevo on the afternoon of April 1, 1876 —at a time when that man had definitely been dead at least ten hours.

The captain sat there in the consul's office feeling a slow chill creeping through his body, and the characters on the paper in his hands dissolved into a picture of the funeral and all its attendant gruesome circumstances. They could not have made a mistake. The man was certainly dead. The burial had not been a hasty affair, for it was undertaken with a proper thorough examination. As it was the first time that he had been in charge of a funeral on his own ship, Wroughton had determined to be extremely careful of every move. Because of this he had not delegated any of the details of examination to anyone else. He had inspected every circumstance connected with the death himself and could have sworn at the judgment seat to the fact that Sherrie was dead. In addition to this, there had been evidence that usual rapid decomposition in the tropics had unmistakably begun before the final ceremony at the gangway.

Nevertheless, there was the name in front of him!

Abraham Sherrie

The captain might have been mistaken in minor details of the signature, but the use of printed capitals followed by a left-handed script was such a peculiar characteristic that it could scarcely be repeated by two different men. As he sat there attempting to make sense of the mystery, suddenly he recalled the statement made by his crewman after the burial, that the corpse had slipped out of its ballast and was rising to the surface again. Poor Captain Wroughton felt the blood rush to his head in a fierce flood of confusion, and soon his mind was whirling around at a rate that was too much for him; he knew no more.

When the captain came to again, he was lying on the sofa in the consul's inner office. Bentwick was sitting by his side, wiping Wroughton's forehead with a cool wet towel. "What's the matter, Captain?" said the consul. "What could possibly have caused you to faint?"

"I don't really know," answered the captain of the *Caribbean*. "I am a deeply confused man, and I would appreciate your indulgence for a few moments."

"Just lie there for a little while. I have business in the office."

Alone again Wroughton went over in his mind every phase of the strange situation. He walked to a chair at the window where there was a fresh easterly breeze and sat down. Then he again recalled the corpse slipping away from its ballast and coming to the surface. What if the body had actually been alive! But these thoughts confused him again, and the blood rushed back into his head until the fierce flood almost panicked him again.

At that moment the door to the office opened, Bentwick entered the room in company with another gentleman whose military bearing identified him as a member of the British Army. The consul smiled.

"Hello, Captain Wroughton. I trust you feel better. May I present my friend, the colonel?"

"It is a pleasure," replied Captain Wroughton, rising.

"I am Abraham Sherrie, but you will excuse my left hand," the army officer volunteered. "It requires an explanation. I served under Sir James Outran in 1856 at Lucknow, and the next year was stationed at Meerut when the mutiny broke out. That year our native soldiers surprised us and I was lucky to escape alive. Unfortunately, before the engagement ended a native soldier wounded me severely in the right arm. Later it had to be amputated."

Captain Wroughton had been listening carefully to the colonel's story, and when the latter had finished he stood up.

"Will you do me a favor, Colonel?"

"Of course, anything you say."

"Would you hand me that document on the desk, Consul?" Robert Bentwick picked up the paper and handed it to the captain. Finding the exact location on the document which he held in his hand, the captain faced the colonel.

"Is that your signature, Colonel?"

"Of course it is. I am Colonel Abraham Sherrie. I landed here with such a bad fever that I preferred the regular attendants at a hospital to the tricky treatment I might get at a hotel. I finally weathered the sickness two weeks ago."

"Well, Colonel, do you know anyone who writes just like that?"

"No, of course not. Or rather, yes, by Jove! I knew one man who stole five thousand pounds sterling by forging my name. He evidently practiced writing my name until he could sign his signature at the bottom of my checks. He originally served fairly well on my logwood plantation in Honduras. He was a queer ugly fellow, with a contraction of his lip, but smart as a steel trap. In his day I suppose he had been a little of everything, and I did make his acquaintance right here in St. Thomas. He had a very convincing manner as you can well imagine, for anyone who hits me for five thousand pounds was not born yesterday. He cleaned out my bank account in Belize

while I was in England last year, and as far as I know cleared
out on a coaster for St. Petersburg after that. I came across his
track in Aspinwall last spring but haven't heard of him since."

The riddle was solved. Casting about for any name but his
own, the mysterious seaman had taken one which he knew and
had forged. Nevertheless, there was one part of the story which
always bothered Captain Wroughton. Why had the man he
buried at sea signed on as Abraham Sherrie? Wouldn't almost
any other name have done just as well?

14

A SEA MYSTERY

The mysteries of the sea are many, but the story of the man who left the ship *Restless* by raft in the night is one of the more unusual ones.

On the outward voyage the ship touched at the Isle of France.* Captain Frederick Johnson announced that as soon as he had gone ashore, if all was well, others might be allowed to follow him.

The next day everyone was allowed to visit this delightful island. Several of the men went up into the hills to explore the area, and one of them, an English sailor named Joseph Carmichael, overstayed his leave. When he came back, Carmichael cheerfully accepted his punishment, which was of a relatively mild nature.

He told the others that he had met an attractive girl, the daughter of an island chieftain. She had taken him far from her native village and shown him a very unusual bird, which she called the "doudo." †

---

* Now known as Maritius, the island is located about 550 miles due east of Madagascar, which is off the east coast of Africa.

† When the first men to go ashore at the Isle of France discovered that the dodo was unable to fly, the bird became an easy victim for hungry men. They

Finally came the day of departure. Farewells were said, and the *Restless* soon left the island far behind. That night, the customary storytelling and singing took place after the change of watch, with the sailors seated upon boxes or sea chests in the forecastle Joseph Carmichael elaborated on his island conquest, and convinced many of the others that life there would be very easy if one could ingratiate himself with the tribal chieftain and marry the daughter in whom Joseph was interested. By contrast, the rough treadmill life he and his associates were leading seemed dismal.

As Joseph talked, the others could sense the longing in his voice as he described his dream girl. Again and again he emphasized the delights of the island which was rapidly getting farther and farther away.

After the watch below had joined in the song "Rocked in the Cradle of the Deep" all turned in, to dream of home and loved ones. At midnight Carmichael went with others to relieve the watch on deck. It was a clear still night with scarcely a breath of wind, and no sound was heard save that produced by the sails as they lazily flapped to and fro accompanied by the dull monotone of the ropes running back and forth in the blocks.

As the red streaks of morning were at last painted on the eastern sky, the relieving watch below was called, but Carmichael had disappeared.

The man at the wheel, it was then learned, had not been relieved by him. Search was at once instituted, but no trace of him could be found anywhere on the ship. The mate

---

devoured its flesh with such relish that within a relatively short time it was extinct. The time the chieftain's daughter showed Carmichael the bird is the last reported incident of the dodo bird's existence.

The dodo was a cumbersome bird, larger than a swan, of heavy, awkward build. It had short, thick, scale-covered legs with three toes before and one behind. Its giant head and enormous bill, the upper mandible longer than the under, was hooked at the point, which made it grotesque in appearance.

sharply questioned the watch, thinking that violence could have accounted for the sudden disappearance of Carmichael. In every nook and corner of the ship, both above and below, the men looked, but without result. One sailor went into the forecastle to renew investigations, and upon opening the chest of the missing man found that his best clothing and some books were gone. He reported his discovery to the captain. Another sailor said that Carmichael must still be aloft, but the thought, doubtless, did not occur to him as to what the Englishman could possibly want with his books there. Nevertheless, the sailor was not satisfied until he had gone up to the foretop and maintop and searched thoroughly.

At this juncture the ship's carpenter made his appearance to report that two of the heavy planks and several joists which he had taken up on deck for repairs the day before were missing. Here was another and more promising clue.

It was now definitely settled that the man had constructed a raft on his watch and had noiselessly lowered it over the side of the ship and made good his escape. This theory was substantiated by pieces of rope which were found near the location of the missing planks.

The foolhardy embarkation of Carmichael on the wide ocean with but a few planks between himself and death seemed appalling to his shipmates. They held various and conflicting views.

One said that Carmichael was "gone on a woman" on the Isle of France, and that he had escaped from the ship hoping to get back to the object of his adoration.

Another believed that the reading of fictitious works had turned the missing sailor's head and made him crazy. The third "spokesman" advanced an apparently more reasonable theory—that Joseph had gone to seek his fortune and a life of ease among the natives on shore, and cited, to strengthen his point, the missing man's desire to marry the chieftain's daughter and thus rise to fame and importance.

When the sailmaker announced that a fragment of tarpaulin had disappeared, it was agreed that Carmichael must be drifting and sailing back to his lady love. Captain Johnson was unwilling to proceed on his voyage until all hope of finding his missing seaman was gone, hence he ran "off and on" during the entire forenoon before he gave orders to square and brace up the yards and make sail for his destined port.

About six months after the incident the *Restless,* on her return voyage, made the port of Sumatra to see if any tidings of Carmichael had been heard.

From the American consul it was learned that a man bearing his description, but who gave his name as Brown, had been found soon after Joseph's disappearance by some boatmen at a point along the coast. Entirely stripped of his clothing, the sailor was in a nearly starving condition. He said that he was a castaway and related his experience with the natives. Preparations were being made to kill him when he made his escape.

As no American vessel was in port at the time, the consul had sent the sailor to Holland on a Dutch ship. Nothing more was ever learned of Joseph Carmichael, the English sailor who left the *Restless* at sea in the night on a raft.

15

CAPTAIN ANDREWS

When I was attending Harvard University I met Woolfrey Middleditch, an Englishman with whom I soon struck up a deep friendship. First he became interested and then amazed at my preoccupation with the sea, shipwrecks, and lifesaving. Two years before I met Woolfrey I had been the lifeguard at the world's largest natural indoor swimming pool, located at Helena, Montana, and he later learned from my mother that I had participated in a series of rescues.

One day in particular, the fourth of July, 1928, I had saved five persons, three of them at one time. Although he never came out and said so, he accepted Mother's story of the rescue with a little hesitancy, especially when she explained to him how I walked along the bottom in eight feet of water pulling three people who had gone down together until I had them in water four feet deep. Several years later, after I had taken a dive from the roof of the Winthrop Yacht Club into relatively shallow water, and on another occasion had swum 207 feet underwater, in his presence, he finally accepted the probability that what my mother had said about me had been based on fact. Later he told me of a book about a really great lifesaver, which he had stored away.

After returning to Ontario, Mr. Middleditch searched for the lifesaving book. One day I received a message from him that it had been written by Captain W. D. Andrews, who in his long career had saved almost fifty persons from drowning. Mr. Middleditch, a professional photographer, had toured Ontario around the turn of the century selling painted enlargements of pictures. One of his contracts was to enlarge and tint a photograph of Captain Andrews. He had purchased a book about the captain from Andrews himself, who had become blind. Years later Woolfrey Middleditch found the volume in a trunk at his headquarters and mailed it to me.

I read Captain Andrews' account with care, and without hesitation offer him as one of the outstanding lifesavers of all time. His feats of daring heroism approach those of Boston Harbor's Captain Tewksbury, who lived at Deer Island, and the world-famous rescuer Joshua James of Hull, Massachusetts.

After many years of research in which at times I despaired of ever compiling a relatively complete account of his career, I am now able to record the story of Captain Andrews.

He first attracted international attention in December, 1886, when the *Buffalo Sun Express* of the tenth of that month contained an article about him. From that date until his retirement he received attention almost yearly.

Captain Andrews was born in the city of Kingston, Ontario, May 19, 1853. Early in life he became fascinated by swimming in Lake Ontario, and it is said that from the age of five he improved his knowledge of the sport. When sixteen years old, he made his first rescue.

At work in a building on July 23, 1869, Andrews noticed a boy of eleven playing on a raft opposite the city. Suddenly the lad fell into the water. At the moment, Andrews had been writing in an upstairs office. He took in the situation at once, ran down the wharf and plunged in without bothering to remove his clothing. The boy was underwater, but Andrews went down, located the youth, and brought him to safety.

When news of his rescue became known, he was awarded the Gold Lifesaving Medal.

In the fall of 1869 he became a sailor on a merchant vessel. Soon the sixteen-year-old boy received his first promotion. His devotion to duty and thorough seamanship gave him rapid advancement, and by 1873 he had become an officer on the Royal Mail Steamer *Waubuno*. While she was lying at her mooring on the west side of the Sydenham River in Georgian Bay, he saw from the deck an elderly man who was attempting to cross the river on a floating timber. The regular swing bridge was under repair at the time, and the man was late for an appointment.

When he was in midstream, the man fell off into the icy water and began a desperate struggle for his life. Diving instantly into the river in all his clothes, Captain Andrews swam out to the drowning man and caught him just as he was sinking. Fastening his grip on the victim's shoulders, Andrews started to the Owen Sound side of the river with him, landing him safely.

Since he was unable to procure a boat to return to the steamer, and although his clothes were beginning to stiffen from the frosty air, he plunged into the ice-cold water again and swam back to the *Waubuno,* where he was received with cheers by the officers and crew. Later the Owen Sound Gold Lifesaving Medal was presented to Captain Andrews for this act of heroism.

In the year 1874 Andrews moved to Toronto, where he soon became known for his ability as an outstanding swimmer and lifesaver. On July 10, 1878, he saved the life of William Waghorne, a twenty-seven-year-old Englishman, who weighed 198 pounds. Waghorne had been bathing in the River Don when he found he was over his head. The water was twenty-seven feet deep. His brother and several companions made many frantic attempts to reach him and then called for assistance.

Captain Andrews heard the cry for help, ran to the scene, plunged in, and saved the man. Later, in addition to being personally rewarded by Waghorne, Andrews was awarded a gold medal by the city of Toronto.

On July 29, 1881, after many other rescues, he swam out to the assistance of two young men near Hanlan's Point and brought both men, about five hundred yards distant, safely to shore. For this brilliant act of heroism he received the bronze medal of the Royal Humane Society and a certificate of honor.

On September 5 of that same year Captain Andrews was awarded the Gold Cross of Valor in recognition of his many daring acts of bravery in lifesaving. This award was presented to him in the city hall in the presence of a large assembly.

Year after year he added to his honors until the total number of people Captain W. D. Andrews had saved approached fifty.

On September 25, 1882, Andrews plunged into Toronto Bay to aid a young man who was seized with cramps and in danger of drowning. Captain Andrews brought him safely to shore. For this act of heroism Toronto's Mayor McMurrich presented him with the Royal Humane Society's bronze clasp and certificate of honor before a large group of people gathered at city hall.

Captain Andrews, together with Island Constable Ward, organized the Toronto Harbor Lifesaving Crew to man the lifeboat transferred from the Harbor Trust to the dominion government, under the control of the Minister of Marine. This crew was instrumental in saving a large number of persons from drowning. From time to time their services were suitably rewarded by the dominion government with binoculars, medals, and clasps from the Royal Humane Society.

During a tremendous storm on July 27, 1883, exceeding in violence anything that had been seen on Toronto Bay for many years, Captain Andrews, with William Ward and John D. Patry, accomplished another rescue. With the storm at its height the three brave men put out in an open skiff at the imminent risk of their lives to rescue Professor Schlochow, a German music teacher whose boat had capsized in the storm. The professor was clinging to the keel while every wave washed over his head. Unfortunately his fiancée, a beautiful, talented young lady named Miss Lauretta Mendon, drowned after Professor Schlochow had made several unsuccessful attempts to rescue her.

In their efforts to reach the sinking man the stroke oar was broken, throwing the boat into the trough of the sea. The next wave filled her completely, forcing the lifesavers to run ashore at Sandy Point to empty her.

Undaunted, they dragged the craft across the peninsula where Andrews and his friends launched her again into the foaming waters, and after terrific exertion they were successful in reaching the capsized craft. Taking off the drowning man, they placed him in the bottom of their boat and pulled for the shore again.

Because of the fury of the gale they were obliged to run before it out through the eastern gap into Lake Ontario, eventually landing on the side opposite the shelter after a pull of nearly three miles.

Over five hundred persons watched the rescue, which is still regarded as the most remarkable feat of lifesaving in Toronto Bay history.

The storm, according to official reports from the Toronto Observatory Meteorological Office, registered wind speed at eighty miles an hour. The enormous seas often hid the boat so that she could only be seen from the shore as she rose buoyantly upon the crest of the waves. The heavy rainstorm which accompanied the wind added greatly to the perils of the situation.

On August 5, 1885, Captain Andrews plunged into Toronto Bay with all his clothes on to rescue a young lad named Edward Lawson. Burdened with the weight of his clothing and his boots, Andrews was forced under by the boy, who was nearly as large as the captain.

Holding his breath, he rose to the surface with the lad and struck out for the shore, retaining his hold of the victim until both were safe. Subsequently Captain Andrews received suitable acknowledgements from the rescued lad, his companion, and the Honorable William Smith, Deputy Minister of Marine. For his conspicuous gallantry on this occasion he was recommended for the Albert Medal.

Thirteen days later Captain Andrews plunged into the waters to save a little girl near the same place and under somewhat similar circumstances. His gallant conduct was reported to the Royal Humane Society by several eyewitnesses.

The captain rescued a woman from drowning in the bay near the Toronto ferry wharf on August 25, 1884, despite the fact the woman had become hysterical. After considerable difficulty he managed to free himself from her desperate clutches. Catching hold of her long hair, Andrews towed her ashore in safety.

On July 1, 1885, together with Constable Ward, Captain Andrews went to the assistance of four persons whose small boat had capsized on Lake Ontario, a mile and a half from the eastern point of the island. After a long hard pull they reached the scene of the accident and found that a large number of boats had collected, one of which contained the unconscious bodies of two survivors, Miss Ethel Mountstephen and Mr. Frank Otter.

They were then taken in tow by the lifesaving crew. Immediately upon reaching the shore all were taken to Ward's

Hotel, where Captain Andrews put in operation the rules of the Royal Humane Society for the restoration of the apparently drowned. In less than half an hour he had succeeded in restoring them to consciousness. Miss Mountstephen and Mr. Otter were able to leave for their homes that same evening.

Captain Andrews received a Christmas present from the young man which bore the following inscription:

> To Captain W. D. Andrews,
> In grateful remembrance,
> Frank J. Otter.

On August 11, 1885, Andrews, fully clad, jumped into the waters near the Wiman Baths and saved a boy from drowning. Both parents of the boy were present.

After eighteen years devoted to the saving of lives, Captain Andrews became blind. His affliction was brought on by exposure to weather and water because of his many lifesaving services. He was presented a handsome gold-headed cane on January 23, 1890. He died in the year 1903.

Never before or since in the history of Canadian lifesaving has any other person even approached Captain Andrews' record.

16

WRECK OF THE *SIBLEY*

For a relatively long period of time the United States government and lifesavers in general had little or no faith in the gasoline engine boat for use in rescue work in time of shipwreck. Finally, in 1907, an amazing performance off the shores of Cape Cod by a gasoline boat brought national recognition and eventual acceptance.

Many New Englanders old enough to recall the era of the 1890's remember vividly only the Portland storm of 1898 and forget a terrible gale that roared in from the sea in October, 1907.

Early on Monday, October 7, the 140-foot three-masted schooner *Charlotte T. Sibley* was off the mouth of the Bass River, Cape Cod. Built in 1885 at Belfast, Maine, the *Sibley* had weathered many a hurricane in the following twenty-two years.

Aware of the gathering storm, Captain Hatch, her master, had sent his anchors rattling down about two miles from shore to ride out the coming tempest. Minute by minute the intensity of the wind increased. Then, at eight o'clock, the cook ran into the cabin where Hatch was eating breakfast and told him that the port anchor chain had vanished. The captain now knew he was in for trouble, because when a storm gets strong enough to break the chain of one of two anchors lowered, it is almost inevitable that the other chain, left to do double duty, will soon part as well.

Nevertheless the second chain held for such a long time that the men began to hope it would stay until the storm subsided. Then shortly after ten o'clock it parted.

The *Sibley,* caught in the blustery southeast gale, started drifting toward shore. Suddenly she struck bottom with such a jarring blow that several of the crew were knocked flat on their faces. Fixings were soon torn away, and the riggings broke free. Chaos was everywhere, but for the moment the masts held.

Now in relatively shallow water, the *Sibley* was still too far out for the men to hope to reach shore unaided. The only boat was filled with water and leaking, and they were almost a mile from land. Each sea, as it roared in from the southeast, smashed against the hull of the schooner, breaking completely over her.

By now the wind was whistling through the rigging at about seventy miles an hour, and the crew had taken to the shrouds. The nearest lifesaving station was at Monomoy, almost twenty miles away, and Captain Hatch realized that it was a hopeless thought that they might be rescued.

Then those on the *Sibley* noticed a small craft coming out of the mouth of the Bass River evidently heading for them. It appeared tiny as the great billows battered it, but it was approaching nearer and nearer toward the doomed schooner.

"I soon saw it could not be a life crew, for there were but five figures in it," Captain Hatch said later. "Soon it was seen to be a powerboat of some sort. Then I realized our chances of rescue rested on a volunteer crew. It felt good to watch that plucky little boat coming closer. How she ever held her course, I will never know."

What was the situation that caused this brave group of five men to start out on their rescue attempt? It all began when Charles Davis, a summer resident of South Yarmouth and an expert yachtsman, received word that a schooner was on Dogfish Shoal, located about a mile out from the Bass River east jetty.

Captain Davis realized that the schooner was likely to break up at any moment and knew that several men were clinging to her rigging. Within a short time he had notified his first mate, Leonidas E. Taylor, his engineer, Otto Stiefel, and two others, Eben B. Chase and Albert B. Pierce, that he was planning to go out from his pier near the House of the Seven Chimneys in his gasoline boat *Ildico* and make an effort to rescue the crew.

Soon all five men were ready. The craft started out into the short reach of the Bass River which lies between the east and west jetty. The wind at the time was due southeast, with a seventy-mile force tearing off the tops of each wave, filling the air with spindrift. But the forty-foot gasoline-engined *Ildico* reached a point outside the breakwater without incident and then entered a dangerous area in the trough of the sea. At times the propeller raced clear of the water. A moment later the boat sat on her stern, the bow aiming directly up into the air. Each time, however, under the careful steering of Captain Davis she headed up on her course and plunged into the "triphammer graybacks" with perfect maneuvering.

Now the schooner was only half a mile away, appearing as a vague blur in the flying spray. Slowly the *Ildico* closed the distance. Literally clawing her way through the smother, finally the boat was just a hundred yards from her goal.

The *Sibley* had struck Dogfish Shoal with her stern at an angle to the seas, which then were wracking her in terrific fore and aft plunging floods of clear green water up and over her hull. Even above the roar of the breakers could be heard the sharp, disheartening sound of splintered wood.

Captain Davis now brought the *Ildico* in so that she was headed directly toward the schooner. He struggled to steer her close under the lee of the wreck, but he realized that any attempt to bring her up directly beneath the stranded hull would result in the *Ildico*'s swamping and all on board being lost.

As he stood by with the *Ildico* splitting the breakers on her sharp bow, he received a shout from the *Sibley* indicating the shipwrecked sailors were planning action. Soon an anchor was lowered over the bow, but nothing more resulted. Almost every wave battered the schooner, carrying with it some fragment of cargo, deck furnishings, or bits of rail.

A half hour passed, and still the motorboat hung into the seas, awaiting an opportunity. Almost an hour had elapsed when suddenly the wind, which had been coming southeast, veered to south. It was the moment for which everyone had waited. The seas changed their direction and now gave Captain Hatch and his crew a chance to act.

There was a small jolly boat aboard the *Sibley* which had been hauled up against the foreshrouds. Captain Davis struggled to his feet in the bow and motioned to Captain Hatch to get the small boat over and allow it to drift down on the *Ildico*.

Unfortunately the men aboard the *Sibley* were in no condition to carry out this difficult maneuver, and instead of going over the stern, the natural place of departure under such conditions, Captain Davis noticed with horror that the men were going to try to get into their boat from the bow. They almost smashed the frail craft to bits against the sharp cutwater of the *Sibley*, but finally the boat was streamed.

Three of the schooner crew now began to lower dunnage into the tossing boat, and at this insane delay those on the

Ildico shouted for the schooner crew to forget their belongings and think of their own lives, for the wind was beginning to change again.

The seven sailors now slid one by one into their boat. Finally they cast off. Once, twice, three times they tried to push off from the bow, but the seas held them. The fourth time they were successful, and their fast-filling jolly boat rolled and plunged on its journey down to the waiting *Ildico*.

Time and again the surging billows ten and twelve feet high completely hid the craft, and on at least one occasion they never expected to see it again. But up and over the boat came to them, nearer and nearer.

Leo Taylor stood holding a line above his head.

"Now!" shouted Captain Davis and the line whistled through the air. It fell true, but was not grabbed by the sailors in the jolly boat.

"Again!" cried Davis.

The boat was now drifting on. In a moment she would be out of the schooner's lee and hopelessly engulfed in the breakers. The rope flew out. Again it was missed.

"Again!"

The third try failed. But as the line drifted by the boat, a survivor pulled it in with an oar and made it fast.

Within a minute the rowboat was hauled alongside the *Ildico,* and one by one the crew of the *Sibley* clambered aboard. Captain Davis cut the boat loose, hauled up his anchor, and swung around on a course which would take him back inside the Bass River breakwater. It was a thrill-packed twenty minutes until they reached a point abeam of the west jetty, but finally the *Ildico* was inside the jetty and the fight was won.

Reaching Captain Davis' pier, the crew was taken ashore and given first aid treatment. Later the residents of the Cape went aboard the wreck of the *Sibley* and rescued the ship's bell and a lead line, which for many years were in the studio of the beautiful Davis home in South Yarmouth.

Without question, the success of Captain Davis and the *Ildico* in rescuing the crew of the *Sibley* finally convinced the government to adopt gasoline-propelled surfboats in its lifesaving service.

The bell of the *Sibley,* according to Theodore Frothingham, is still preserved on the banks of the Bass River in the House of the Seven Chimneys.

17

CAPTAIN LOUIS DOUCETTE

One of the most unusual men of his generation, eighty-five-year-old Captain Louis Doucette, now living on Cape Cod, Massachusetts, has participated in many remarkable adventures. It could be said that his life has had at least four periods of high excitement, the first occurring in the year 1910 when he was one of the heroic crew of five to go to the aid of the stricken schooner *Mertie B. Crowley.*

The second came in 1918, when a U-boat sent to the bottom the fishing craft on which he was sailing 225 miles out to sea from Highland Light, Cape Cod. The third was a day in November, 1919, when a terrific explosion shattered his schooner *Gleaner* and killed four of his crew. The fourth was during Prohibition when he was engaged in rum-running.

I visited Captain Doucette at East Falmouth several months ago, and he told me the story of his life.* I was particularly interested in his account of the *Crowley* rescue.

During my visit to this famous sailor-fisherman I told the

---

* Captain Doucette had five daughters and three sons. One of his boys was lost at sea aboard the *Doris Gertrude* out of New Bedford. In addition to his son, the *Gertrude* carried his son-in-law and nine other men to their doom. Three boats were fishing together, and one of them, the *Gertrude*, disappeared. Nothing was ever learned of the craft. She simply vanished.

captain that every time we pass over Martha's Vineyard aboard the Flying Santa plane, in which I deliver presents to lighthouses each Christmas season, I like to come down over Wasque Shoals because of the remarkable rescue in which he participated there in 1910. At that time the area was the scene of one of the most spectacular events in Martha's Vineyard history. Today Captain Doucette is the only living survivor of those rescuers who went to assist the ship's company of the *Mertie B. Crowley.* Captain Doucette told me in 1965 that chances against all aboard the *Crowley* being saved were a thousand to one. His leader was a brave, reckless, Cuttyhunk-born, Edgartown fisherman named Captain Levi Jackson, and the operation he directed achieved a special place in the annals of shipwreck history.

The *Mertie B. Crowley* was the largest and longest schooner ever launched at a Rockland, Maine, shipyard. Although 412 feet from jibboom to spanker, at the waterline she was just 300 feet.

During the two years following her launching the *Crowley* enjoyed a period of prosperity. Then one night in 1909 she collided with a barge off Highland Light. The barge had to be beached, but the *Crowley* continued her journey. After repairs she went back into service. Another mishap occurred in December, 1909, when she stranded on the dangerous Tuckernuck Shoals. Freed later, she proceeded without incident to her destination.

On Friday, January 21, 1910, the *Crowley,* under the command of Captain William H. Haskell, aboard with his wife, was off Long Island, carrying a cargo of 4,850 tons of coal. There was a thick haze. At five thirty on the morning of January 23, the captain sighted a light, actually Edgartown Light, shining across the sand dunes. He mistakenly believed he had seen the lighthouse high on the southern cliffs of Block Island. Suddenly, without warning the schooner ground to a halt on what proved to be the northern end of Wasque Shoal, Martha's Vineyard.*

Mighty waves hit the *Crowley* and began to slide up over her side onto the deck. Captain Haskell shouted down to his wife, "Come on, Ida, we've got to get into the rigging," and he helped her climb the shrouds.

Almost from the moment of stranding, Captain Haskell realized that the *Crowley* was doomed. The seas from the snowstorm were still rushing in and over the sands of the shoal, and the vessel had gone well into the reef.

Back in Edgartown thirty-two-year-old Captain Levi Jackson was alerted by his neighbors. Master of the little thirty-seven-foot power sloop *Priscilla,* he had made a reputation for himself as a fearless seaman, and because of this the people of Edgartown that morning started a pilgrimage to his home to find out what he could do.

Captain Doucette's statement to me follows:

I was the first one of the crew that knew about the wreck that morning. I was always there bright and early and made coffee aboard the *Priscilla.* Some young fellow came running down and told me about the wreck. One of the crew was the first to notify Levi. Finally we got under way and went out. We had a sixteen-horse engine. We had sails set going out. It was very rough. I still recall the awful foaming mass of surf and waves.

* Captain Doucette told me in 1965 that an irregularity in the light may have confused Captain Haskell, causing the wreck of the *Crowley*. Doucette had called the government's attention to the light discrepancy earlier that week.

Aboard the six-master the survivors on the mast had watched the forward part of the schooner break off, with the forward house lifted up and carried away. Immediately afterward the *Crowley* snapped in two amidships. Soon the jigger, driver, and spanker * masts began to sway and twist at dangerous angles. Then those people on the schooner noticed that Captain Jackson had run the *Priscilla* up under the lee of the *Viking*, which had also ventured offshore as a possible source of help.

Watching for a favorable chance to sail across, Jackson suddenly found the sea conditions which he wanted and began his gamble. Time after time he shot the *Priscilla* out into the rough waters; time after time he was in danger of being capsized by the billows but managed to outmaneuver them.

Reaching a point about half a mile west of the *Crowley*, Captain Jackson worked his way in † closer to the schooner.

Finally there remained a bare two hundred yards, the trickiest and most dangerous waves of all to negotiate, those on the shallow shoal around the *Crowley* herself. Levi Jackson knew that if he made one false move the crowds on the shore would soon be picking up his own lifeless body and those of his crew.

It was a wild scene. Relentlessly, towering billows continued to break. It seemed sheer foolhardiness that anyone would try to brave such a sea. Then for a moment Jackson thought he saw his chance. Shooting the sloop ahead, he slid her just under the crest of a moderately large comber. Unfortunately, in a split second the billow built up at once to gigantic proportions and headed for the *Priscilla*. Levi brought his craft

---

* Masts were fore, main, mizzen, jigger, driver, and spanker.
† Contrary to the usual story told on Martha's Vineyard, Doucette says the spray that day did not freeze on either vessel or on the people involved.

around, maneuvering straight for the twelve-foot peak about to break. Just before the crest began to tumble, the *Priscilla* slid over the ridge and down the smooth seaward side of the billow.

He had saved the *Priscilla* by the narrowest of margins, and the closeness of the escape shook him. Reaching a point a hundred yards away, he decided to run for the *Crowley* from a new angle. He started but suddenly changed his mind. When he came back a second time, he found conditions were more favorable and steered the *Priscilla* to a position almost under the *Crowley's* stern.

Ordering the men to make ready the anchors, he let go both of his bowers. He was now secure. The next move was to put out the three dories, a man in each boat, with instructions to row slowly but steadily toward the *Crowley*.

"Pat and Henry and I manned the dories," reminisced Captain Doucette in 1965. "Gene stayed on the *Priscilla* with Levi. Kelly got Mrs. Haskell. I got six of them. I made seven trips. I rescued Pat Kelly, one of our own crew, who nearly drowned. Pat got in trouble when Cook Whalen of the *Crowley* jumped at the wrong time and landed in the water. When the cook grabbed at the dory, over it went, and Kelly and Whalen found themselves struggling in the water.

"I rowed to them. One came up, Patrick Kelly, and I rowed closer and got him. We then pulled in Whalen. He was big and heavy. I rowed back for another one and got the cabin boy. At first he wouldn't jump. 'Jump, you son of a gun, or we'll leave you,' we yelled at the cabin boy. He was very small, my gracious. His name was Charlie Bridgewater. We brought them all into Edgartown."

Carnegie Medals were later awarded to all five men.

Abridged accounts of the awards follow:

⚓

Award No. 551. Levi Jackson, aged thirty-two, fisherman, helped to save William H. Haskell, aged forty-six, sea captain; Ida M. Haskell, aged thirty-four; and twelve others from drowning, Edgartown, Mass. In a very rough and treacherous sea, following a heavy storm, Captain Jackson and a crew of four men went in the *Priscilla,* a small fishing boat, to a disabled schooner which had grounded on a shoal in the Atlantic Ocean, four miles from shore. The *Priscilla,* after careful maneuvering, was brought in the lee of the schooner and anchored. The *Priscilla* had to make a trip of thirteen miles, part of the way through very heavy seas, to reach Edgartown, a huge wave at one time nearly filling the boat. *Bronze Medal and $2,000 to be applied to his debts, and other worthy purpose, as needed.*

No. 552. Patrick S. Kelly, aged twenty-two, fisherman, helped to save William H. and Ida M. Haskell, and twelve others from drowning, Edgartown, Mass., January 23, 1910. Kelly manned a dory and made five trips to the wreck, rescuing Captain Haskell and three members of the schooner's crew. *Bronze Medal and $1,000 for a worthy purpose, as needed.*

No. 553. Louis A. Doucette, aged thirty-two, fisherman, helped to save William H. and Ida M. Haskell, and twelve others from drowning, Edgartown, Mass., January 23, 1910. Doucette made seven trips to the stranded schooner in a dory and rescued six of its crew without mishap. *Bronze Medal and $1,000.*

No. 554. Henry A. Kelly, aged twenty-four, fisherman, helped to save William H. and Ida M. Haskell, and twelve others from drowning, Edgartown, Mass., January 23, 1910. Henry Kelly, a brother of Patrick, rowed four times to the wreck, taking off the Captain's wife and three members of the crew. *Bronze Medal and $1,000 for a worthy purpose as needed.*

No. 555. Eugene L. Benefito, aged thirty-seven, fisherman, helped to save William H. and Ida M. Haskell, and twelve others from drowning. At Captain Jackson's command he remained on the *Priscilla* and with him helped the benumbed and exhausted shipwrecked ones from the dories to the deck. *Bronze Medal and $1,000 toward purchase of a home.*

"I don't think I was scared during the rescue," Doucette told me. "I was concerned in the first of it, but as soon as we got people going I was right at home."

Captain Doucette used his share of the Carnegie award money toward the purchase of his fishing boat, the twenty-eight-foot sloop *Gypsy Maid.*

"My father made a small fortune in that small boat and had many experiences," Margaret Harney, his daughter, told me. "He fell overboard one time and was almost drowned. He was in the water almost an hour before the cook, who was deaf, noticed him."

In 1918, Captain Doucette had a thrilling adventure with a U-boat on Georges Banks. As he tells it: "We were 225 miles southeast of Highlands, Cape Cod Light, that August. We had seventeen swordfish which we got the day before aboard the *Progress.* We saw the U-boat in the morning. She was right on top. The U-boat skipper said, 'We would have got you yesterday, but the fog bothered us.'

"They did not fire. We were stopped. We were hard at

work when they said, 'Get into your dories and make your course Nor'west.'

"We took two dories and rowed way. Mattie Richards was in one and I took the other. Mattie was lost for two or three days.

"The dory that Mattie was in didn't have anything with them, no water, no provisions. They just took off. But the U-boat sank the schooner.*

"They sank seven or eight boats by shooting a gun mostly. We got across the banks. We made the schooner *Acushnet*, a fishing boat, thirty-two hours later. They brought us in to Boston Harbor. Aboard the *Acushnet* there were many other survivors of ships sunk that day."

Doucette now "bought into" a large schooner which he sailed out of New Bedford. Built at Rockport, Massachusetts, she was called the *Gleaner*. He owned her in partnership with Allen Waddell. Three years later he bought out Waddell.

When he first had the *Gleaner* in 1919, he made three trips in her. One day in November she was loading gas from the foot of a gas station off 69th Street, Bayridge, New York. Suddenly there was a dreadful explosion, and the schooner was blown apart. Four of her crew lost their lives. Captain Louis Doucette, of New Bedford, suffered a broken arm and burns about the body. Eugene LeBlanc, of Boston, was burned severely by the explosions.

There had been three separate explosions in quick succession. Persons along shore said that the first one seemed to shoot the vessel through the water until she was twenty or more feet from the floating gasoline station. The second explosion sent the vessel completely out of the water and hurled her crew overboard. The third blast shattered the ship, with the burning wreckage floating off toward the Narrows. Badly

* Nine years later the German government paid for the wartime sinking of the *Progress*.

injured, Captain Doucette spent close to two years in the Marine Hospital at Staten Island.

"After that," explained Mrs. Harney, "he came out of the hospital. The boat was raised, reconditioned, and in her he made other trips. He was going along perfectly fine into Boston Harbor with a load of fish when off Point Allerton he hit submerged wreckage, and the *Gleaner* sank. She had a brand new engine in her that he had just bought. He lost everything from then on. He didn't have enough insurance on her to pay. It really was the end of his sea-going days for a while. However, it didn't daunt him, and he later went into running rum.

"The skipper was hard up, and fish were very cheap, so he was really forced into rum-running. He made about five trips off the coast of Cape Cod. They would go out in the schooner *Isabel Q.*, make contact with the rum ship, pick up their load, and deposit it on the Cape beaches. The captain and his oldest son, Captain Louis, Jr., were in a raid down on Nauset Beach. They loaded $84,000 worth of rum."

Captain Doucette was quite frank concerning his rum-running days.

"They finally caught us just inside Cape Poge Light and towed us to Woods Hole. In Boston we were put on probation, all but one man. They confiscated the boat and $40,000 worth of liquor. We were fined in federal court. The second time we unloaded off the beach at Nauset. The schooner would go out and contact the rum ship, take the load off, bring it in off the beaches, and they would row out in dories. One of the Coast Guard men was to be paid off, and he suddenly decided not to accept the bribe."

The skipper of the Coast Guard station turned in the alarm, and the rum-runners were caught, but Captain Doucette, his son, and another man who was one of the "big wheels" in the outfit got away.

"Some of the fellows fainted," his daughter relates, "because the Coast Guard started to shoot, and they got so scared they thought they were shot and fainted on the beach. But Captain Doucette and two others hid in the bushes and got away from the Coast Guard. There was $84,000 worth of liquor. They had to row out to the boat and load it in the dory, and row back in and dump it on the beach. They had beach-buggies."

Margaret Harney added that her father "would have gone to jail if it had not been that Prohibition was repealed, and the charges were dropped. Father needed some money, and I called Boston one day, and they said to me, 'Who is this?' and I said, 'It's Pop's daughter,'—they called him 'Pop.' I had been down to the place they had on the Cape in Mashpee, and they had huge trucks that were bringing this stuff back and forth. I saw the whole layout. They had a camp. They were really tough people. They told me in no uncertain terms to forget what I had seen. He got the money, but they never did pay the fines."

18

⚓

NEW ENGLAND SPY MYSTERY

At least three U-boat landings along the Atlantic Coast took place during World War II. Two of them are relatively well publicized. One, which is called the Amagansett Landing, took place in June, 1942, near Amagansett, Long Island, about 105 miles from New York City. The other occurred in Florida not far from Jacksonville. These two U-boat landings have been reported fully by Allen Hynd in his *Passport to Treason* and by Colonel Vernon Hinchley in *Spy Mysteries Unveiled.**

As far as is known, however, there is no publication in any book regarding a New England incident when two men landed from a U-boat on the Maine coast in the year 1944. American-born William C. Colepaugh and Eric Gimpel, a German national, came ashore in a rubber raft from Nazi *U-boat 1230* at Hancock Point, Maine.

Actually, the FBI records on one of the spies went back several years. William Curtis Colepaugh had been under the

* A Cape Cod World War II landing from a U-boat was revealed to me recently by C. Graham Hurlburt, Jr., of Cohasset, Massachusetts. The landing was said to have been on West Dennis Beach between Lighthouse Inn and the entrance to Bass River. German radio equipment was later found there, according to this information.

observation of the FBI for some time. In June of 1940 an FBI special agent in Boston was informed that customs officers had observed Colepaugh from May 2 to May 27, 1940. During that time he visited the German tanker *Pauline Friederich*, which was tied up at Battery Wharf in Boston.

The customs official stated that Colepaugh claimed he was engaged as a painter aboard the vessel. He often spoke, while visiting the German tanker, of going to Germany to study engineering. It was also reported that he expressed dissatisfaction with conditions in the United States and was interested in leaving this country.

It occurred to the customs officials that because of Colepaugh's dissatisfaction with conditions in the United States the FBI might wish to conduct inquiries concerning him. Thus a case was opened on William Colepaugh, and instructions were issued to make the necessary checks to determine whether or not he was engaged in subversive activities.

Investigation revealed that William had been a student at Massachusetts Institute of Technology where he studied naval architecture and engineering. The records of this school showed that he entered in September, 1938. He had attended a secondary school in Toms River, New Jersey. His home address was listed as Niantic, Connecticut, with his birth as March 25, 1918.

Because of scholastic difficulties, Colepaugh left the institute on February 6, 1941. The name of one of his former roommates was obtained from the authorities at MIT. This young man advised the government that William often received mail containing propaganda publications from the German consul in Boston and also from German news agencies in New York. He indicated that Colepaugh showed more than ordinary interest in these publications.

Customs guards stationed at the wharf where the *Pauline Friederich* had been docked remembered Colepaugh. One guard indicated that William claimed he was living on board the *Pauline Friederich*. When asked if he were a crew member of that ship, he replied that he was not but lived on board because he liked the crew members.

Another customs guard said that he stopped Colepaugh on one occasion when he was attempting to board the ship and asked him what his business was on board the vessel. William replied that he had permission from the chief officer to spend a few days aboard the *Friederich*. When asked by the customs guard why he wanted to go on a German ship, Colepaugh replied that the persons on board the ship were treating him well and he liked them better than the people in the United States.

A retired customs guard was located, and he related that he remembered seeing William in the company of the first officer of the *Pauline Friederich*. He said he also had seen him in the dining room with the captain of the ship.

The FBI learned that in August, 1940, William Colepaugh had two German sailors from the *Pauline Friederich* as weekend guests at his home in Niantic, Connecticut.

In June, 1940, Colepaugh's address was unknown. One individual advised that William might be in South America as a crewman aboard a merchant vessel. It was not until fourteen months later that he again attracted the attention of the FBI.

One afternoon in August of 1941 a young midshipman from the United States Naval Academy walked into the Field Office of the FBI in Washington, D.C., and reported that he had roomed with an individual named William Curtis Colepaugh at a secondary school in New Jersey from September, 1937, to June, 1938. He indicated that he was anxious to let the FBI know about Colepaugh. He said that he went to visit William in March, 1940, at the Massachusetts Institute of Technology. During this visit Colepaugh took him to the German tanker, *Pauline Friederich*, and it appeared that William was well acquainted with the officers on board that ship. As they were leaving the ship, Colepaugh told the young midshipman that he was in favor of Germany and that he wanted to go to Germany on the *Pauline Friederich*.

The midshipman further related that in June, 1940, William came to visit him in Groton, Connecticut. During the course of a walk, they discussed the war. Colepaugh was asked where his affiliation would lie if the United States went to war against Germany. His reply was that his affiliation probably would be with Germany.

This young midshipman stated that he never had an occasion to meet Colepaugh after this incident, but what William had told him bothered him. He felt that because of Colepaugh's attitude toward Germany, the former MIT student should be investigated.

All this time the FBI was building up data concerning Colepaugh. Information was received that he had either sold or given a radio receiving set to a former attaché at the German consulate in Boston. Reportedly, William had built this set himself.

Information was also received that Colepaugh was a frequent visitor at a German tavern frequented by members of the German consulate in Boston. On one visit to this tavern William stated that he had just returned from England on a British freighter.

On July 23, 1942, the *Scania,* a Swedish vessel, arrived at Philadelphia from Buenos Aires. The crew list of that vessel indicated that William Colepaugh was a seaman aboard her. Colepaugh was questioned by local naval officers, at which time he presented a Selective Service card indicating that he had registered under the provisions of the Selective Training and Service Act on October 16, 1940. During this interview he admitted that he had not communicated with his local draft board, and explained that he had never received any communications from that board. This information was immediately turned over to the government, and Colepaugh was interviewed by FBI agents.

The FBI office in Philadelphia communicated with their Boston office, resulting in a check of the records of the local draft board in Boston where Colepaugh had registered. It was found that he had failed to return a completed questionnaire to that draft board and had also failed to keep the draft board advised of his address. Of course, these were violations of a federal law under the investigative jurisdiction of the FBI. Accordingly FBI agents in Boston contacted the local United States attorney. On July 25, 1942, a complaint was filed against William C. Colepaugh charging him with violating the Selective Training and Service Act. A warrant was issued for his arrest.

William was returned to Boston, where he again was interviewed by agents of the FBI. He said that he was born at East Lyme, Connecticut, and claimed that his father was a native-born American. His mother, however, was born aboard the German ship *The Havel* while she was en route to the United States. He explained that it was while he was a student at Massachusetts Institute of Technology that he met the captain of the German tanker, *Pauline Friederich*. Through this meeting he was invited to visit the ship and did so on several occasions. During these visits he became acquainted with a man whom he knew to be a Nazi party leader on board the vessel and on two occasions took this party leader to the Colepaugh home as a guest.

William said that he had purchased a radio set and that subsequently he received a telephone call at Boston from the secretary to the German consul who was interested in the radio. Colepaugh denied building the set but admitted selling it to the German official for sixty dollars.

Colepaugh stated that he had visited the German consulate

in Boston on numerous occasions during the early part of
1941.

He said that from January to April, 1940, he was employed
at Lawley's shipyard in the Neponset section of Boston as a
laborer on yachts. Three men were in charge at the shipyard.
Edward Whiting was the superintendent, Frank Payne was
the second in command, and Bror Tamm was third. William
was believed to have been hired by Payne.

Colepaugh is remembered as a thin, mild-mannered youth
and a dreamer, but no one who is now living remembers him
at the time as being a person who would attract more than the
average amount of attention.

At this period Quincy resident and yacht builder Bror
Tamm was directing work on the yacht *Wildfire,* a steel
schooner. She had been built in 1923 in Bristol, Rhode Island,
by N. G. Herreshoff. In 1932 her owner was Horatio Hatha-
way of Boston. Colepaugh is believed to have worked on the
Wildfire and on the yacht *Constellation.*

Bror Tamm well remembers the *Constellation.* A tremendous steel craft 135 feet long, she was designed by Edward
Burgess and built at City Island in New York in 1889. Her
owner in 1932 was Herbert M. Sears, and her home port
Marblehead.

One of the officials at Lawley's in the year that William
Colepaugh worked there told me in February, 1965, that
Colepaugh probably was one of the men who left the yard at
once on hearing that he would have to be fingerprinted and
photographed.

"Several men left in a hurry on learning this information,
not even stopping to get their pay," my informant explained.

On May 7, 1941, Colepaugh went to Canada and shipped
out as a seaman on the *Reynolds.* The boat went to Scotland
and returned to Boston in the latter part of July, 1941. William subsequently landed in New York City. On September 5,

1941, he obtained a job as a deckhand on board the *Anita,* which left New York City for Rio de Janeiro. He was at Buenos Aires in October of 1941. On December 8, 1941, the day after the Pearl Harbor attack, Colepaugh secured a position as deckhand on the tanker *William G. Warden.* He made a few trips on this craft in South American waters, and on March 25, 1942, he was again in Buenos Aires. On April 5 of the same year, he worked as a deckhand on board the *Scania.*

Colepaugh stated that he had written to the German Library of Information in New York City for publications, and he added that he had attended a birthday celebration in honor of Hitler at the German consulate in Boston. The secretary to the German consulate, according to William, had discussed with him the possibility of his going to Germany to study at various marine engineering schools in that country.

The United States attorney in Boston advised that he would not authorize prosecution in the case against Colepaugh if the latter would enlist for military service. Colepaugh promised to do this.

On October 2, 1942, William enlisted as an apprentice seaman in the United States Naval Reserve. Since he became a member of the Armed Forces, under the jurisdiction of the Navy, the FBI's case on William Curtis Colepaugh was closed administratively. Copies of FBI reports in this case were furnished Navy officials for their assistance.

On June 28, 1943, the FBI received information that William had been discharged from the Navy "for the good of the service." Once more he was in civilian life, and again the FBI began to interest itself in his activities.

On March 26, 1943, Colepaugh commenced employment at the Waltham Watch Company at Waltham, Massachusetts, and a little over three months later, on July 7, 1943, he was known to be working for a poultry farmer in Concord, Massachusetts.

A check with the local draft board indicated that Cole-paugh had telephoned them on January 10, 1944, that he was going to enter the Merchant Marine and would send a letter to his local board advising them of his exact employment. Five days later, the draft board received a letter from William postmarked New York. Enclosed with this letter was a note on the stationery of the Swedish American Steamship Line certifying that he was employed on board the *Gripsholm* as a messboy.

The FBI had been informed that the *Gripsholm* was carrying individuals who were to be repatriated to Germany. It was not known whether or not Colepaugh would return to the United States as a crew member aboard the same ship. The FBI therefore placed notices with several government agencies so that these agencies would advise the FBI in the event Colepaugh returned to the United States.

On February 15, 1944, the *Gripsholm* sailed. Within a few days of her arrival in Portugal, Colepaugh looked up the telephone number of the German consulate at Lisbon. He made a telephone call to the consulate but was advised that the consul was not in. At noon of the following day William went to the consulate in person and told the doorman that he was from the *Gripsholm* and wanted to see the consul. Colepaugh explained that he was a friend of the former German consul at Boston.

Within a relatively short time William had been interviewed by the German consul in Lisbon and taken to Germany. He was then transported to the headquarters of the Security Service at The Hague in Holland. Here he met Eric Gimpel, who now began training with Colepaugh for the dangerous mission ahead, a mission which would include crossing the Atlantic in a German submarine and landing on American soil.

Colepaugh's courses included training in radio work and

use of firearms and explosives. He was given a tremendous amount of athletic training to build up his relatively weak body, and he learned to drive a motorcycle. He was taught how to handle explosives and shown the most effective way to derail a train. He was given training in handling thermite, which could burn through metal. Above all, he was told never to be afraid of explosives.

Gimpel's record was an excellent one for the task ahead. He had been an instructor in 1943 at a Fascist academy in Madrid, Spain, for young boys, after which he returned to Berlin as a prominent member of the Security Service. In Berlin he had been given a private office and a secretary.

In August, Colepaugh and Gimpel went to Berlin where, using a Leica camera, they were given a photographic course including developing and printing special photographs. Then they went to Dresden, Germany, where they studied microphotography and learned to work with microphotographic apparatus. They soon were able to reduce regular Leica negatives to 16 mm. film, and then they returned to Berlin.

When he was in Dresden, Colepaugh did not know what his assignment would be, but later he learned that they were to go to the United States. Two days before William and Gimpel left Berlin for Kiel they were advised that their objective in the United States was to obtain information from periodicals, newspapers, radio, and all available sources regarding shipbuilding, airplanes, and rockets. Gimpel was to build a special radio which would send information out of the United States. In an emergency they were to use American prisoners of war as "mail drops." Letters sent to these mail drops were to be written in secret ink. In sending radio information out of the United States, they were to use specific code-wave lengths and times.

After final intensive training in every department of espionage, Gimpel and Colepaugh were assigned to early transportation by submarine to the United States on the *U 1230* and sent to Berlin.

Their final instructions included the code for sending messages on the radio to Germany. It was based on the words "Lucky Strike cigarettes, it's toasted." They were also furnished wrist watches and two small compasses. They were given two kits of concentrated food which had been taken from captured American pilots.

Gimpel received a blue onionskin paper packet containing about one hundred small diamonds which were to be used to provide funds in the event the money given to them was found to be worthless or dangerous to use.

The day before Gimpel and Colepaugh left Berlin for Kiel they signed various identification papers which were later turned over to them in Kiel. The papers made out for Colepaugh carried the name William C. Caldwell. These papers consisted of a birth certificate showing Colepaugh to have been born in New Haven, Connecticut; a Selective Service registration card showing him to be registered at Local Board 18, Boston, Massachusetts; a Selective Service classification card from the same draft board; a certificate of discharge from the United States Naval Reserve; a motor vehicle operator's license for the state of Massachusetts; as well as several duplicate papers, completely signed and filled out except that names and addresses were omitted to permit Colepaugh and Gimpel to assume other names if such was found necessary.

About September 22, 1944, Gimpel and Colepaugh went to Kiel where they spent two days waiting aboard the Hamburg-American liner *Milwaukee*. Subsequently, they went aboard German submarine number *1230*, which evidently was ready to depart from Kiel. The submarine left immediately and remained off Kiel for about two days waiting for a German convoy going up the coast of Denmark. They proceeded with this convoy to Horton, Norway, where the submarine was

given tests for about six days. They then went to Kristiansand, Norway, where they remained for two days, taking on
food and fuel.

Colepaugh and Gimpel had received $60,000 for their ex-
penses. This sum had been determined when Colepaugh had
pointed out that the cost of living in the United States had
taken a sharp turn upward. He estimated that it would be
necessary to have $15,000 a year for the living expenses of one
man in the United States. Based on this estimate, the $60,000
was given to them as expenses for two men for a period of two
years.

On October 6, 1944, the submarine left Kristiansand and
proceeded out into the broad Atlantic, bound for the United
States. The trip across was made under conditions of extreme
caution.

On November 10, 1944, the Nazi submarine approached
the Grand Banks of Newfoundland. At that point, the crew
took radio bearings on Boston, Massachusetts, and Portland
and Bangor, Maine. Later they established a position off the
Maine coast at Mount Desert Rock. They lay off that point
until about 4:00 P.M. on the afternoon of November 29, 1944.

During the day the submarine rested on the ocean bottom.
During the night it charged its batteries by using its Diesel
engines. Through listening devices the crew were able to hear
fishing boats on the surface nearby. Throughout one day they
had listened to a fishing boat which was anchored above them.
About this time word was received by radio from Berlin that
a submarine had been sunk in Frenchman's Bay, Maine, and
the captain of the *1230* was instructed to land Colepaugh and
Gimpel somewhere other than Frenchman's Bay.

William, Gimpel, and the captain * of the submarine discussed other landing places in Rhode Island, New Hampshire,

* The captain of the *U 1230* was H. Hilbig. He surrendered his U-boat
June 24, 1945, at the period when many others were giving up.

and Maine. The captain, however, disregarded the instructions from Berlin. On the night of November 29, 1944, the submarine, completely submerged, started for Frenchman's Bay.

About one-half mile off Crab Tree Point the captain ordered the craft to be raised until the conning tower was just above the water. In this fashion they proceeded to a point about three hundred yards from the shore at Crab Tree Point, which is near the peninsula of Hancock Point.

During the trip across the Atlantic, Colepaugh and Gimpel had worn regulation German naval uniforms; but about half an hour before the submarine came to its offshore position, they removed the uniforms and donned civilian attire.

The submarine turned to face the south, and the crew made ready a rubber boat with oars. Attached to this boat was a light line to be used to pull the rubber boat back to the submarine after Colepaugh and Gimpel had rowed ashore.

When the rubber boat was launched, the line broke, and it was necessary for two crew members to row the agents to the shore, so the sailors could retrieve the boat. At the landing point there was a narrow beach of approximately six feet, with a bank above it.

In the stillness of that cold November night on the Maine coast, Nazi agents Colepaugh and Gimpel stepped from the rubber boat onto the shores of the United States. The German sailors also went ashore so that they could return to Germany and brag that they had touched the shores of the United States. When these sailors departed they saluted, "Heil Hitler."

In possession of all their equipment, William and Gimpel climbed the bank and walked through the woods adjacent to the shoreline until they reached a dirt road. They did not bring any explosives ashore nor did they bury anything on the beach. In fact, they did not even bring the microphotographic apparatus from the submarine because it was extremely heavy. Gimpel claimed later they were weakened because of their long stay aboard the submarine.

On that night of November 30, 1944, five months before VE Day, Colepaugh and Gimpel came up a path leading through woods to the road which runs along the west side of Hancock Point. After they started on foot down the road toward Hancock, two Americans soon became aware of their presence. One was Mrs. Mary Forni, wife of a Franklin, Maine, schoolteacher, and the other was an Ellsworth High School senior Harvard M. Hodgkins.

Mrs. Forni, the mother of three children, was driving the family automobile home from a gathering of neighborhood women. It was shortly before midnight and there was a moderate snowstorm.

A little later, on another spur of the point-encircling highway, young Hodgkins was driving home from a dance at Hancock Village. Mrs. Forni recognized the Hodgkins car. She had also seen two men laden with bundles walking along the high road. She noted that although the men were strangers there was apparently nothing suspicious about their actions.

However, after Mrs. Forni reached home she began to wonder why two strangers should be trudging along late at night in the Hancock Point area at that time of the year. If it had been July or August at the height of the summer season, she wouldn't have "given it a second thought."

The more she thought about it the more it worried her, and finally Mrs. Forni decided to call the Hodgkins' residence the following morning. The lad's father, Dana Hodgkins, a deputy sheriff, was away on a hunting trip. Mary Forni talked with Sheriff Hodgkins' wife on the phone and asked her to question her son regarding the two men. Harvard confirmed their presence by saying that without question he had seen the tracks of the men along the road as he drove home.

That afternoon Deputy Hodgkins came home and began an investigation of the incident. He followed tracks in the snow down a path at Hancock Point to the water's edge, where he saw enough to convince him that the men had landed from the sea. At first he wondered if the pair could not have been hunters, but when he saw that the tracks ended at the ocean's edge and there still was evidence that a rubber raft had been landed, he decided to get in touch with FBI representatives in Bangor.

Four days after the landing the FBI questioned Mrs. Forni and the Hodgkins boy and set in motion machinery for the eventual capture of Colepaugh and Gimpel.

As part of his usual duties Hodgkins had been carefully checking the area for strangers at the time, with special emphasis on possible breaks into homes of summer residents, and had also been assisting Naval intelligence when possible.

Harvard, because of Boy Scout affiliations, spent a whirlwind week in New York, as a guest of a New York newspaper and the manager of a radio program of that era.

In recalling the incident Mrs. Mary Forni stated that it was one of the big thrills of her life. "It was exciting when it happened. My husband was unconcerned but I was tremendously thrilled. When the FBI came in to talk to me, I was indeed surprised."

She put the incident out of her mind until almost everything about the men's capture was revealed at the close of 1944. The story continually cropped up at her house year after year.

These are the people who helped make history on that memorable night in 1944 when one of the most daring spy plots hatched in World War II came to an end—before it ever got started.

Although the two spies did reach Boston, and later New York, Colepaugh decided to surrender, and did so. He aided in the capture of Gimpel, after which both were sentenced to be executed as German spies.

Their sentences were changed, and later they were allowed to go free after serving a substantial number of years in prison.

When I visited Mrs. Forni recently up on the Hancock Point peninsula, she took me across to the very location where the four Germans from the *U 1230* landed on the beach.

"It all seems like a dream, today. Of course, more than twenty years have gone by, and time has its way of affecting all of us. But I'll never forget that night when I saw the two German spies hiking along that snow-covered road. I knew that something was very, very wrong. Under normal conditions, they simply would not have been there!"

19

THE *ENCHANTRESS* VANISHES

On Veteran's Day, 1963, a stranger walked into the Duxbury Boatyard off Washington Street, Duxbury, Massachusetts, and talked for some time with the manager, Captain Frank A. Davis. He was interested in purchasing a substantial yacht but found nothing there which suited his fancy at the moment. Captain Davis then walked with the visitor across to his car.

"If you find the type of craft which you want, I'd be glad to sail her for you wherever you wish to take her," Davis said in farewell.

About a week later Captain Davis received a long-distance call from New York. It was the stranger, John L. Pelton, an insurance man from Whittier, California, who had purchased a yacht named the *Enchantress* on November 17. He was calling to remind Captain Davis of his half-in-earnest promise to sail the craft which Pelton might buy. The captain agreed to take the *Enchantress* with the provision that he would be permitted to return home for the Christmas holidays. Accompanying him would be the owner Pelton, forty-seven years old.

Captain Davis arrived in New York, met Mr. Pelton, examined the *Enchantress,* and decided to employ as crew a nineteen-year-old boy named Brad Miller, who obtained consent for the trip from his father, who was in Puerto Rico at the time.

The *Enchantress,* had been built at the Bath Iron Works, Maine, in 1925. Her length overall was 59 feet (at waterline 50.5 feet); her tonnage, 20; her beam, 12 feet; her depth, 7.5 feet; her horsepower, 20; and she was designed by Cox and Stevens.* Her home port in 1956 had been New York, while her owner that year was Edwin J. Dresner.

For yachtsmen who would appreciate a detailed description of a sailing craft, I include the following:

The *Enchantress* was a schooner of composite construction, with steel frames in her bottom as well as wooden steam-bent frames with 1¾" mahogany planking fastened on by means of copper rivets. She had teak decks, while her trim was all mahogany and teak. Her designers had given her a short bowsprit and good spars, although they were not exceptionally heavy for an off-soundings boat. Fourteen tons of lead were fastened to her bottom. For sails she had several good dacron and nylon staysails, with some exceptionally good fore staysails, two poor cotton mainsails and a storm mainsail. There also was a queen, a spinnaker, and a fisherman. For auxiliary power she had a small four-cylinder Gray marine engine with a reduction gear and a two-bladed propeller. In good weather, her auxiliary power could carry her at seven knots. A radio direction finder and a radio ship-to-shore telephone had been installed. She had a teak hatch forward of her mainmast and an opening in her galley just aft of her foremast. The skylight in her main cabin was about three feet by two and a half feet in size. The *Enchantress* carried more than the necessary amount of life jackets, and they all had an approved Coast Guard tag.

* Other names by which the *Enchantress* had been known include *Flytie, Clytie, Ahyee, Sea Bride, Dominica, Wydowe, Rexanne.* At one time she was owned by B. Devereux Barker at Marblehead.

She also carried an eight-foot fiberglass round-bottom boat. There were buoyant cushions but their condition was not satisfactory. A life belt was always handy which would buckle around a person's middle; the six-foot lanyard on it had a heavy bronze snap which could be clipped to the rigging when going forward or working on deck to prevent one's being lost after falling overboard.

After many hours spent in inspecting the *Enchantress* in drydock at Fife Shipyard, Glen Cove, New York, Mr. Pelton listed needed items, obtained them, and made final preparations for a sea voyage. Captain Davis repeated his willingness to sail until Christmas time, when it was agreed that he could return to his Duxbury home to spend the holidays.

On November 28, Thanksgiving morning, the newly conditioned *Enchantress* sailed from Manhasset Bay, New York. Although the thirty-eight-year-old craft was heading south with seasonal wintry weather approaching, both Captain Davis and the owner thought they had a good chance of reaching Florida without serious trouble. However, it is only fair to state that Davis was interested in unstepping the masts and going most of the distance by inland waterway, while Mr. Pelton, who had no idea of the terrors of a wintry Atlantic, had dreams of sailing beyond soundings once warmer climes were reached.

On the journey from New York to Charleston, Davis took the boat on the inland waterway and went as far as he could inland. Soon a decision would have to be made. He wanted to remove her spars, lay them on deck, so that he could go by inland waterway all the way to Florida. He suggested this possibility to Mr. Pelton, who emphatically told him no. He would not allow the captain to take the masts out of the boat. Davis definitely believed that at that time of year it would be safer to go on the inland waterway rather than to sail around Cape Fear with such a small vessel.

The *Enchantress* was soon offshore, proceeding south. Captain Davis eventually guided her into Chesapeake Bay and then to Norfolk, Virginia, taking the inland waterway to Morehead City, North Carolina.

After a final conference at Morehead City between the owner and the master, they ran to Southport, South Carolina, on the Cape Fear River with bad weather all the distance. Two attempts were then made to leave Southport, but on both occasions the weather forced them back.

Finally, on the third attempt, the *Enchantress* sailed outside. The storm that bothered them had southeast winds from thirty-five to fifty knots, bringing substantial seas which at times were from eight to ten feet high.

The *Enchantress* behaved very well during the windy, rough weather. While Captain Davis was aboard, no appreciable amount of water was ever taken in from the seas, although when pounding hard in heavy weather, she took on a small amount. Under way at sea, she maneuvered nicely, although with the propeller coming out through the port quarter she was an awkward vessel to handle under power, especially leaving a dock.

When Captain Frank Davis had inspected the *Enchantress* at the dry dock in Glen Cove Landing, New York, he found the vessel in satisfactory condition for a boat as old as she was. Her interior was rather poor, with the plywood fittings in need of repair, but her masts were in good condition. There was one plank on her port side forward on her waterline about six to eight feet long which had to be replaced. The rudder post was very good. She had a bilge plug which was given a lead patch to prevent it from ever coming out. The shaft log through the counter was in reasonably fair condition, while the stuffing box had been repaired when the *Enchantress* was in dry dock.

The owner of the boat had limited experience in small boats, mainly powercraft. He did have a small eighteen-footer used for water skiing around Long Beach, California, and on the Colorado River. His knowledge of sail, however, was gained only through reading books. He had never handled or sailed a craft of the *Enchantress'* size. A brilliant man, Pelton had more than an average amount of common sense. While on the trip, he was constantly asking questions of Davis, building up his knowledge of the sea. John Pelton was just unable to understand how weather on the East Coast could change so rapidly, with the result that he was extremely skeptical of what he was told. He had a hard time appreciating the fact that one could sail from beautiful calm weather into a bad southeast storm in a matter of fifteen to twenty minutes.

The *Enchantress* sailed by Charleston on December 13. Then the weather became so dirty that Captain Davis decided to turn back and entered Charleston Harbor. During this period they had used both sail and engine, but with the emphasis on sail, starting the auxiliary only when necessary. They then tied up at the City Dock where the dockmaster agreed to watch over the craft.

While in Charleston, John Pelton decided to leave the *Enchantress* and go by bus to Miami where his wife and the boys were awaiting him. All hands were to leave the *Enchantress,* which was still tied up at the City Dock. Brad Miller left the boat here, and Frank Davis traveled by bus with Pelton to Miami, where it was decided that the famous Polish adventurer and sailor Count de Grabowski would relieve Davis, who was then free to go home to Duxbury to spend his Christmas holidays with his family.

Count Christopher de Grabowski, a veteran trans-Atlantic "loner," had crossed the ocean from Tangier to New York a few years before in his twenty-five-foot cutter *Tethys* and was vice commodore of the Slocum Society.* The count had logged at least fifty thousand miles under sail between 1958 and 1963. A devoted lover of the sea, he was the ideal solution to John Pelton's problem of obtaining another good captain for the *Enchantress.*

Shortly before sailing, Count de Grabowski wrote to the magazine *Motor Boating* a letter which appeared in the March 1964 issue:

> Dear Editor:
>
>   . . . I hope to sail on January 7 or 8 directly for St. Thomas, some 1200 miles distant. I shall be skippering *Enchantress,* a pretty fifty-nine-foot schooner on an extensive voyage—six months and 8000 miles. Her owner, who will bring his wife and two sons along, is a southern California insurance man completely new to yachting.
>
>   We sail from Charleston to California via the Windward Islands and Panama. I'm looking forward to this trip for we also hope to visit the Galapagos, Cocos and above all Clipperton Atoll which is seldom seen by yachtsmen.
>
>   Chris de Grabowski
>   Charleston, S.C.

On January 7 Captain Davis talked from his Duxbury home by phone with Pelton, who had returned to Charleston and was then expecting to leave within a short time. Those then living aboard the *Enchantress* were Pelton and his wife, the two boys, and Count de Grabowski.

The schooner sailed from Charleston, South Carolina, under the command of Count de Grabowski on Friday, January 10, 1964. Her destination was announced as St. Thomas in the Virgin Islands. The beautiful blue craft was soon hull down off the Carolina shore.

---

* Honoring Captain Joshua Slocum, who sailed singlehanded around the world.

On Monday, January 13, a distress call came from the *Enchantress*, which had run into gale winds off Florida.

When he received the May Day call from the schooner, Radioman C. C. Leonard of the Coast Guard Jacksonville Beach Station requested the *Enchantress* to give a long count so that shore stations would have the opportunity to pinpoint the location of the ill-fated craft.

The official Coast Guard findings,* completed on July 28, 1964, include the information that the distress call of the sinking *Enchantress* was estimated about 150 miles south southeast of Charleston. A second report eighteen minutes later revealed that the water in her cabin was knee-deep.

"A man started the long count," explained Leonard later, and then he heard a child's voice continuing the count. It counted on and on for at least ten minutes. At the end it was very weak, and then it faded out altogether.

Immediately upon receiving the distress call, all available search and rescue units were alerted. At 1945 (7:45 P.M.) January 13, search aircraft were on the scene conducting an illumination search. The air search continued until sundown January 17, using as many as six Coast Guard, seven Navy, and one Air Force aircraft at one time.

In Coast Guard parlance, at 2315, 13 January, the search by surface vessels commenced, with the *USS Franklin D. Roosevelt, USS Perry, USS Power, USCGC Sweetgum,* and the *S/S Esso Baltimore* taking part. The search extended from latitude 30° 20′ N., longitude 78° 30′ W., over an area of twelve thousand square miles.

The search results were generally negative. However, several pieces of flotsam which included a boat cushion found in latitude 30° 45′ N., longitude 78° 28′ W., were later identified at the Charleston Marina, Charleston, South Carolina. Donald Hesse and Nathan Chaplin stated the cushion was

* Coast Guard Files ORB-2/20922.

one they had seen aboard the *Enchantress* while she was at the marina prior to sailing for the Virgin Islands.

The conclusions of the Coast Guard follow:

1. In view of the absence of further communciations from the vessel, and the negative results of a thorough search of the area, it is concluded that the vessel sank on 13 January 1964 about 150 miles south southeast of Charleston, South Carolina.

2. The five persons on board—the captain, Christopher de Grabowski; the owner, John L. Pelton, his wife Linda Pelton; and their two sons Dean Pelton and Dale Pelton—met death due to the sinking.

3. It cannot be ascertained just what caused the vessel to sink, but the weather conditions at the time were a major contributing factor.

As in the case of all craft which disappear at sea, there have been many conjectures on what happened to the *Enchantress*. Although several wild and unreasonable statements have been made, including one which claims she was captured by the Cubans, I believe it is safe to assume that she went down shortly after her final message had been sent to the Coast Guard that stormy day. She sank to the bottom in the middle of the Gulf Stream, and most fittings or materials which may have floated up probably followed the route of the Gulf Stream in the general direction of Norway.

In a heavy pounding she might have lost one of her hatch covers, and her hatches would have filled with water. She could have hit something and poked a hole in the hull. It is possible that her seams started a leak, and if the crew did not watch her bilge, by the time the water was up to her cabin it would have been quite a job to unload what had been taken in. If the gasoline pump was not working, they never could have gained on the leak. Possibly the pounding heavy water may have loosened the planking up around her stem, and her forefoot splice could have opened up.

It is also conceivable that the hull around her toilet fittings might have let go. This does not happen often but in an older boat, which had been up in a boatyard between owners and had dried out, the strains of pounding by heavy seas could well open something. Bror Tamm, yachting expert and former yacht architect, stated that if all hands were on deck the trouble might not be noticed until it was too late.

In the words of Captain Davis, "What happened during the last few hours aboard the *Enchantress* will be a mystery, forever locked in the sea. One must actually sail the Atlantic to appreciate the sudden changes of weather from balmy winds to rough and heavy seas which often occur in a matter of minutes."

The story of the *Enchantress* now joins tales of other craft which disappeared under tragic circumstances.

20

TRAPPED UNDER THE
SURFACE OF THE SEA

In the month of September, 1964, a giant dredge capsized in Australia, trapping twenty-three men below the surface of the sea under circumstances rarely equaled in the marine history of the world. Although eight of the victims died almost at once, efforts were made to rescue the others, who were kept alive by air which had been trapped inside the craft.

In two of my other books * I tell similar stories. In 1846 the sloop *Adelaide* capsized off Barnegat, eventually drifting ashore near the lighthouse there. A hiker along the beach went down to the water's edge and climbed up on the bottom of the sloop. Suddenly a noise was heard, as though a person might be tapping from within the hull. An hour later a hole had been chopped in the sloop's hull, and a terrified girl, Captain Lamson's daughter, was pulled out of the sloop.

Thirty-one years later the schooner *Cod-Seeker* capsized off Nova Scotia with two young boys caught in the forecastle. Samuel Atwood and James E. Smith clung to the bottom of a bunk and breathed the trapped air for no less than 80 hours

* *Lighthouses of America, Strange Tales from Nova Scotia to Cape Hatteras.*

before the overturned schooner was sighted. In this time the *Cod-Seeker* had gone to the bottom. Her salt cargo slowly dissolved, allowing her to rise again to the surface, still capsized. Later she was boarded by rescuers from the American schooner *Matchless,* who at length heard the tapping under the keel and cut a hole to rescue the two boys.

The Australian incident was on a much larger scale and developed into one of the most astounding rescues in Australian history. The disaster which befell the Danish dredge *Kaptajn Nielsen* occurred late in the evening of Friday, September 18. It was not until early Saturday morning that seaman Eric Poulsen, after an incredible four-mile swim followed by a two-mile staggering run on the beach, reached Moreton Island in Brisbane Harbor to report the tragedy and ask for help.

Unfortunately, when Poulsen stumbled up to the first house he could find, the people mistook him for a drunk. Attired in his wet underwear, his feet cold and bleeding, he began mumbling to them in broken English. Finally after he was able to convince his listeners that he was actually a survivor from a weird marine disaster, a massive rescue effort swung into operation.

In a short time the air was filled with police appeals through every radio station in the vicinity begging owners of outboard motorboats, cabin cruisers, and work boats to go out to the scene of the disaster. Sergeant Les Clark of the Water Police notified all civilian skin divers that they were needed desperately.

The response was amazing and gratifying. Dozens of craft, including launches, speedboats, trawlers, and tugs soon converged on the area. The most vital move was made by a scuba diving organization headed by Joe Engwirda, thirty-two, a professional diver who ran a school for underwater divers in Brisbane. Arriving on the scene with the greatest haste,

Engwirda took active supervision of the rescue. It was a situation which no scuba diver had ever faced before. In the middle of the night in pitch darkness under the surface of the ocean the divers explored the overturned craft foot by foot. They discovered, with the help of electric torches, that when the giant dredge capsized, the steel plates had burst in two, and several doors had broken from their hinges. Fighting their way through the overturned craft, Engwirda and the other scuba divers reached the survivors in cabins which were half-filled with water. There was still enough trapped air to keep the sailors alive.

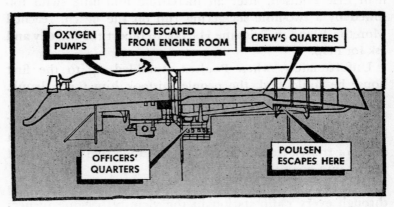

"They were panicky when I first got there," explained Joe, "but I had to spend about a half hour talking to the sailors before I brought them out. Fortunately I speak a bit of Danish.

"We got aqualungs for the trapped men to come up with. I gave the crewmen a quick lesson on using the aqualungs and let each one have a short workout in the cabin before we tried to get out.

"We had to take the men out through a skylight only three feet wide. In the middle of the skylight was a steel bar and we could not get through with our aqualung equipment on. We had to take off our aqualungs to pass through and then put them back on again. We had trouble pulling the men through the skylight. One chap was too fat to get through and he panicked, but he finally escaped. On the average it only took two minutes to get each man from his cabin to the surface. We used air hoses for panicky ones who could not be given aqualungs." Air was also sent into the hull to replenish the supply.

Senior Constable Ivan Adams also covered himself with glory that September morning, bringing up several of the survivors. He said that the "trouble was that most of the trapped men had not used underwater gear before. One of the men refused to use gear at all. I grabbed hold of him, told him to take a breath, and got him out as quickly as possible. The door of a cabin had been smashed and we had to tear it away to get into that particular cabin. We had to rip furniture away from around another man who was trapped in his cabin."

After being underwater continually for more than four hours, the constable collapsed. It was found that he had developed a severe carbon dioxide headache from the impure air in the ship. He and Engwirda had been the first skin divers on the scene. Adams said later that the superstructure and bridge of the dredge were buried in the sand, and the ship was fast on the bottom.

At 2:00 P.M. the afternoon following the disaster Water Police Sergeant Jim Schofield, in charge of rescue work, gave up all hope of finding more survivors and announced the discontinuance of operations. Sergeant Schofield said: "There is definitely no one left alive on board. A dozen skin divers have just searched the length and breadth of the ship. They went into every nook and cranny, every cabin, every alleyway, dining room and engine room. They tapped in each section of the ship, but got no response. Then they repeated the search, just to make sure. They are satisfied there is no person alive aboard the ship."

Sergeant Schofield emphasized the fact that fifteen crewmen escaped. It was "the greatest stroke of good luck I have seen in many a day."

Schofield said that it was his opinion that the dredge had turned over suddenly. "It just went 'whoof.' "

When the tragedy occurred, Sergeant Schofield reported, the dredge was taking on sand and had almost completed a capacity loading.

Sergeant Schofield, who had been on continuous regular duty since 10:00 P.M. on Friday, September 18, first got word of the disaster at 3:05 A.M. Saturday.

Mr. William Isherwood, at the Tangalooma tourist resort, reported to the Water Police that crew member Eric Poulsen had come out of the water and run along the shore to let people in the area know that the great dredge had turned turtle.

"We thought it was a joke, but I checked it out and found the dredge was overdue. We immediately organized rescue operations."

Sergeant Schofield said it was impossible for them to use oxyacetylene equipment to cut through the hull to reach the trapped sailors.

A medical team—Dr. Elizabeth Richards, Dr. Gordon Hawkins, Dr. Ian Morrissey, and Dr. Burnett—gave resuscitation to survivors.

First sign that something was amiss was at 11:30 on Friday night when holidaymaker Bob Anthony was gazing out from the Tangalooma tourist resort. He saw "what looked like searchlights" and a long cigar-shaped vessel in the channel between Moreton Island and the mainland. He dismissed it as a "submarine" and went to bed.

Then at 3:00 A.M. seaman Eric Poulson, his feet cut and bleeding, staggered ashore after his long swim and exhausting run along the beach. Dressed in only his underpants and a polo shirt Poulsen knocked at the door of the cottage of Mr. and Mrs. Noel Bennett.

"Boat overturn . . . Many drown . . . telephone," he said in broken English when Mrs. Bennett answered his knock.

"I thought he was a drunk in the overflow from a party at first," Mrs. Bennett said, "and I was a bit scared, so I closed the door and went to tell my husband. But Poulsen kept knocking and when we had a good look at him we realized something terrible had happened."

Noel Bennett, Frank Adler, and Bill Isherwood set out for the vessel in a small craft. Reaching the overturned dredge, they climbed up on the slanting bottom. When interviewed later, Frank Adler said: "We tapped 'How many are you.' and they tapped nine times."

"Help won't be long," they were told. "Keep your spirits up."

The survivors later related what their thoughts and actions had been while they were imprisoned in the dredge. Electrical engineer Kim Petersen, thirty-six, the last to leave the underwater tomb, told his rescuers the following day that there was no panic. This might be in contradiction to what Joe Engwirda states above, but possibly conditions were different in divided parts of the submerged craft.

"Even when things looked the worst, we were confident you would get us out somehow. I promised the boys that we could stay alive at least two days. Maybe I was a bit optimistic."

Petersen praised the spirit of all the survivors, particularly several young members of the crew. Even when the water was rising and the air getting stale, they kept their heads and managed to tell a joke or two.

"I was sitting on my bunk," said Petersen, "when the dredge lurched over. I managed to drag myself through the cabin door. Just as the lights failed I saw James Madsen, a young Danish apprentice, madly scrambling up the living quarters steps.

"Madsen was met by a wall of water and disappeared. He drowned. I and eight others managed to climb into an upturned cabin that contained a trapped air bubble. When the water settled, clusters of phosphorescent organisms gave us a little light to see with.

"I tapped a chair leg on a table for three hours to let anyone outside the hull know that we were still alive.

"After three hours my prayers were answered when an answering tap-tap-tap rang through from outside the keel. Incidentally, several of the men had been bruised when the barge capsized, and were bleeding; some were worried that the blood might attract sharks.

"All the time we were peering into the water waiting for divers to reach us. It was a terrific feeling when the first frogman came through a skylight under us in the cabin roof."

The first survivor to be rescued was Per Wistensen, a fifteen-year-old cabin boy. He was followed by Gurg Jakobsen, fifty-eight, oiler, the oldest man in the cabin. Aage Hansen also was brought up safely. Petersen, the last one rescued, had volunteered to show young crew members how to use the air equipment earlier.

For the *Kaptajn Nielsen*'s chief cook, Aage Hansen, fifty-two, of Rudkjobing, it was the third time he had been lucky. Hansen, one of the men entombed for eight hours in the flooded cabin, had a previous record of shipwrecks at sea.

Waiting to have a gash on his forehead treated at the General Hospital, Hansen showed a large scar on his right arm. "Mussolini gave this to me when one of his planes bombed our ship out of the water during the Spanish civil war.

"In 1942, during Hitler's war, my boat went down off Greenland after it struck a rock, and we were stranded in Greenland for three months. Nevertheless, last night was easily the worst experience I had at sea. In my bunk when the dredge turned over, I was stunned by a blow on the head.

"One of the cabin doors flew off its hinges and I found myself floating down a passageway. I swam and paddled into another cabin where there was not so much water, and there were my mates.

"The spirit of the boys was wonderful, especially that of the young ones. During the night they sang songs and some even told jokes." Hansen said he would be going back to sea as soon as he returned to Denmark. "It's my living," he asserted.

Dion Jorgensen, seventeen, deckhand, of Aarlborg, Denmark, said he heard three men drown shortly after the dredge capsized.

"They were calling for help, but we couldn't do anything," he said. Jorgensen said nine seamen crammed into his cabin as a wall of water bore down on them when the dredge went over.

"We thought we were going to die," Jorgensen said. "Nine of us stood in water about four feet and a half deep. We were in that room for eight hours."

Rescue from the deathtrap hull came as a birthday present for Gurg Jakobsen, an oiler from Copenhagen. "Today is my fifty-eighth birthday," Jakobsen said at the General Hospital.

Engineroom-hand Christian Reinholdt arrived at the Brisbane General Hospital semiconscious from immersion and shock. Others taken to the hospital were the captain of the dredge, Karl Albert Flindt, and the second officer, Niels Sonne. Reinholdt and Sonne were picked up by helicopter, which landed on the water near the disaster scene.

Piloted by Captain Ray Hudson, the helicopter sped them

to Victoria Park, less than a quarter of a mile from the hospital.

Two survivors, Svend Frederiksen, twenty-six, and Borje Hanson, forty-four, missed certain death by a bare six inches. The first two to be rescued, they had climbed out through a pipe and were sitting on the overturned hull when help arrived.

"In seconds," Frederiksen explained later, "the water rushed in and then all the lights went out. I found myself down in the main engine room, swimming in the darkness. The water was covered with oil from the diesel and lubricating tanks. I swam over to Hanson and we climbed up on one of the engines to try to get out of the water. It was dark and cold and the water was rising all the time.

"I found one of the engine room tools and banged on the hull, but there was no answer. The stern end was getting deeper, so we swam forward. We heard the hissing of air trapped in the compartment escaping. It came from one of the big tubes through which sand is pumped when dredging. We decided to get into the tube. If we opened it and it was full of water we would drown for sure.

"Our air was nearly gone and the water was up to our chests so we risked it and tore it open. We could see the end of the tube about eighteen feet ahead. Most of it was underwater, but the top of the tube was six inches clear. We crawled along it keeping our heads out of the water, then ducked down and swam out. We sat on the keel waving the flashlight but could not attract anyone's attention, though we could see people on the shore. Finally we were rescued."

At the three-day hearing held later in the year professional skin diver Joe Engwirda, in testifying before the shipping inspector, Captain R. Hildebrand, said that he believed the capsizing of the *Kaptajn Nielsen* took no more than ten seconds. He based his opinion on observations he had made while diving into the semisubmerged dredge. Engwirda found that furniture drawers which could have moved to starboard had not had time to slide out of position. He tested the drawers and they moved easily.

He added: "Another reason for my opinion is that the ship filled with water so quickly that a lot of the crockery was still unbroken."

The water came in so fast that when the crockery shifted at the moment the dredge capsized, the dishes fell into water instead of onto the metal deck.

Engwirda said he also considered that from the time the dredge began to capsize to the moment it completely turned over it had not moved more than ten feet from the location over which it was working. He deduced this from the debris which was beneath the ship on the sea bottom.

On the final day of the inquiry Captain Hildebrand listened to testimony on the load meter and the clock from the bridge, but it was impossible to prove anything of importance.

Engwirda said that the engine room telegraph on the bridge was at "slow ahead" for one engine and at "half ahead" for the other. He had seen this when he first dived into the bridge house.

"They have since been moved," he said. "I don't know by whom, but someone must have been playing around with them."

Mr. Engwirda said the covering glass on the load meter was broken "by someone or something" after it was taken from the dredge and placed in a small surface boat.

At the time of the capsizing Constable Ivan J. Adams of the Water Police contacted Mr. Engwirda, and they used Mr. Engwirda's speedboat to reach the scene at about 7:00 A.M. He said the ship was "anchored" in the sand, principally by the bridge, the funnel, and the masts and gantries.

"I did not observe any marks on the hull which might indicate that the ship might have grounded," he added. "Neither did I see any cracked plates or dents on the hull. I also examined the chains supporting the hopper doors. All locking pins were in place, while the ship's suction pipe was still attached. The head of the pipe was also connected and in one piece."

Adams explained that the lifting wires were lying in the sand, but he could see no breaks. Constable Adams added that "on the bridge I saw a series of levers with black knobs. All were in a neutral position except one. This was pulled back," he said. "I could read some inscription which said: 'Use only with key.' There were a considerable number of spare pieces of gear, steel plate, chains, nuts, and bolts lying on the sea bed. I could not see the anchors or cables on the bottom, but the lifeboats were still attached to their davits."

The capsizing of the dredge *Kaptajn Nielsen* has never been fully explained to the satisfaction of the public, and a majority of mariners who studied testimony at the various hearings which took place after the accident agreed that there was much which could never be either proved or understood concerning this strange marine disaster.

Long after other incidents in connection with this tragedy are forgotten, the astounding feat of Seaman Eric Poulsen that terrifying night will be recalled by the people of Australia. His remarkable swim and run along the beach to get aid stand alone in heroism and bravery.

INDEX

INDEX